P9-DVE-406

BEFORE
IT'S
TOO
LATE

A NORTON PROFESSIONAL BOOK

BEFORE
IT'S
TOO
LATE

WORKING WITH
SUBSTANCE ABUSE
IN THE FAMILY

David C. Treadway, Ph.D.

W. W. NORTON & COMPANY • NEW YORK • LONDON

Copyright © 1989 by David C. Treadway

All rights reserved.

Published simultaneously in Canada by Penguin Books Canada Ltd.,
2801 John Street, Markham, Ontario L3R 1B4

Printed in the United States of America.

Library of Congress Cataloging-in-Publication Data

Treadway, David C.
   Before it's too late : working with substance abuse in the family
   David C. Treadway.   —   1st ed.
      p.   cm.
   "A Norton professional book."
   ISBN 0-393-70068-2 :
   1. Family psychotherapy.   2. Substance abuse.   I. Title.
RC488.5.T715   1989
616.89′156 — dc19   88-38922

ISBN 0-393-70068-2

W. W. Norton & Company, Inc., 500 Fifth Avenue, New York, N. Y. 10110
W. W. Norton & Company Ltd., 37 Great Russell Street, London WC1B 3NU

          6   7   8   9   0

Kate, this book is dedicated to you.
You were there before it was too late.

Contents

Preface

It is late September. I have retreated to my boat on the Maine coast — to be alone, and to work on this book.

Last night a cold front came through and for a while it was quite rough in the anchorage. The rain beat on the decks, the wind came in strong, and the boat pitched and rolled. Down below I was snug and warm in my sleeping bag. I listened to the noises of the storm and felt the motion of the boat. I thought of the summer when I sailed across the Atlantic alone. I remembered the cold, creeping fear on a stormy night as I lay in my bunk and listened to the boat crashing through the seas. I would listen for something wrong, for something breaking. I would wonder if I should go up on deck, look around, and check the sails. The nights seemed so long. I would snuggle back down in my bag, waiting for sleep or the first hint of light on the horizon while listening to the rush of the big ones rising up behind me. Last night, on the Maine coast, I remembered the darkness and the waiting and the being alone.

Writing this book does not feel safe to me. It is too personal, too stripped of my normal professional veneer. I care too much about it. It feels risky. It is not like being in a snug anchorage at the end of a pleasant day sail. It has all the potential for both the exhilaration and disaster of a solo ocean passage. I am in the middle of it now. There's no going back. It's been going very slowly lately. I just need to find the rhythm again. The simplicity.

At sea the motion never stops. Slowly your body develops a rhythm with the boat. Slowly your cluttered, busy, demanding world narrows to the simplicity of sky, wind, and sea. Slowly you become attuned to the play of dark and light, the shifting shades of blue, the sunrises and sunsets.

A book called *Ocean Passages for the World* includes charts for the world's oceans with recommended courses for different times of the year and different types of ships. It is a compendium of information about currents, climate, and potential problems along the routes. It does not explain why the ocean works the way it does. It simply addresses the question of how best to plan a voyage so that it will be relatively predictable and safe. Many sailors preparing for an ocean voyage start with this book. They discover early on that, in plotting a course, a straight line is rarely the shortest distance between two points. You have to learn how to anticipate the winds, the currents, and the weather and to organize the trip accordingly. Choosing courses that allow you to sail with the wind and the current are often better even if they seem longer. Sometimes sailing in the "wrong" direction will get you home faster and more safely.

Before It's Too Late is a simple book. It is designed as a useful guide for therapists working with families in trouble with substance abuse. I discuss the many different ways in which this kind of family appears for treatment and then present detailed models for how to work with them in a step-by-step fashion. Some safe and effective treatment courses are charted, with due consideration of the currents and climate. Sometimes the recommended courses will seem to head off in the "wrong" direction; however, my experience tells me that the straight line approach is not always useful.

The book has several significant limitations. It does not answer all the many unresolved questions about the nature of alcoholism and drug addiction, nor does it presume to present the "right" way to do family therapy. It offers neither a detailed description of the alcoholic family system nor a theoretical framework for practicing family therapy. In addition, it does not adequately address the different patterns of substance abuse and methods of treatment that result from the particular drug of choice, ethnicity, gender, and socioeconomic background of the abuser. My treatment models will need to be carefully adjusted to fit the multitude of different substance abuse patterns. Finally, since this book attempts to build a bridge between the family therapy and the substance abuse fields, some aspects of the presentation will seem redundant and rudimentary to each group.

Much of what I have to say is neither original nor brilliant. With an odd combination of modesty and arrogance, I offer this book simply as a description of my way of working with families with substance abuse problems. This is a book about my clinical practice and my own experience of learning by doing. During the 18 years that I have been working with families and substance abuse, I have made a lot of mistakes. I have tried to learn from them; perhaps this book will allow others to learn from them as well.

In approaching the treatment models in this book the most important caveat to keep in mind is that plotting the course is not the same as making the voyage; following a treatment model is not the same as doing the therapy. Therapy is never so neat and simple.

As a novice therapist I attempted to adhere quite rigidly to treatment models in my head. I remember treating a family with a difficult adolescent. Predictably, his parents were divided and cowed. The classical structural family therapy treatment plan called for the therapist to help the parents unite in order to take an authoritative position with the adolescent. Over several sessions I tried to empower the father. Finally the father began to confront the boy. He accused him of having some pot in his back pocket. Naturally the son denied it. I continued the "enactment" by encouraging the father. The father escalated the challenge. The next thing I knew the father and son were rolling around on the floor, with the father trying to grab the pot out of the boy's back pocket. I was frozen in my chair, unable to decide if this tussle was a good thing. When Mom got down on the floor and tried to help Dad contain the kid, I thought to myself, "This is great—the mother and father are working together to take on the kid. I should have this on tape." However, when the boy broke free, stood up, began to take a swing at his father and then knocked over my lamp, it occurred to me that perhaps the session was a little out of control. I tried to speak up, only to discover that I had lost my voice and could only manage a strangled squeak. Finally, I squeaked out that I was going to call the police, at which point the son wisely ran out of the room. The parents collapsed in their chairs. Bathed in sweat and completely out of breath, they were both crying. I was just beginning to comfort them when the boy came back into the room, threw a pitcher full of water on them and then ran out again. The session was not unfolding according to the plan.

Ironically, this disaster was the turning point of the case. The parents and I were thoroughly united by our shared sense of total defeat and humiliation. We began to make some real headway after that session. Some years later I found out that the boy had gone on to become a class officer at his college and generally very successful. Could I have planned such an outcome?

Treatment models are simply reference points that allow us generally to know where we are and where we are headed. The actual treatment is the process of integrating what we see in the family and the model we are using. The model helps us organize the data, pick out what is significant, anticipate responses, and know which steps might be appropriate next. It is an organizational tool, a way of helping us think about our clients, ourselves, and the course of treatment. Treatment models do not help when we are reduced to a squeak.

We therapists practice an arcane art while feeling the weight of the expectation that we should be scientific and objective. No wonder many of us wonder if we are frauds or hypocrites. We look to the experts to teach us and make us wise. We go to workshops and read books so we can feel that we know what we are doing, so we can feel safe. But where do the experts get the answers? They find the answers through years of hard work, constant pondering, and their life experience. The same as we do.

A systemic approach always includes the behavior and motivation of the therapist in the analysis of the therapy. Perhaps the same principle should be applied to teachers and authors, so that the answers they espouse are less intimidating and possibly more useful. Magicians may feel diminished by showing the tricks that do not work along with the ones that do, but that is the way to help others risk becoming magicians.

Describing treatment models and telling other people how they should do therapy are safe parts of this book for me. I teach frequently and I am very good at treating other people's cases. Exposing myself, on the other hand, scares me. It scares me to be open about how sometimes the therapy I do is not at all like the simple treatment models that I teach; to be open about my growing up in an alcoholic family and how much being a therapist is part of my recovery; to be open about how sometimes my needs for intimacy get met in the therapy room, where I am able to be very close to clients and still feel safe; to be open about how sometimes I ask my clients to confront issues that I have been unable to deal with in my own life; and finally, to be open about the tricks that do not work.

The last of the clouds have blown over. The sky is a deep rich blue. It is windy and cold. There is a hint of winter in the air. I am bundled up in the cockpit. My hands are cold. I am squinting at these lines because the sun is so sharp and bright as it reflects off the water. I am trying to see clearly.

Acknowledgments

When I turned 40, my wife, Kate, and my sons, Michael and Sam, gave me a rocking chair and a pillow for me to lean on. The pillow had an imprint of each of their hands on it, symbolizing their support. Throughout the past couple of years I have relied on that pillow. It's lumpy now and needs to be cleaned. Some of the stitching has come loose. I need to take better care of it.

If I had known what writing a book would take out of my life with my family, I might not have done it. Michael, Sam, and Kate made this book possible with their love. Her firm hand and their little hands have supported me while I faced the computer screen. There are no words for how much I appreciate their help. I look forward to the repair work.

In the early seventies I worked at Eagleville Hospital, where I learned how to work with alcoholism and drug addiction. I was also lucky enough to spend several years training at the Philadelphia Child Guidance Clinic and later to become a staff member there. My understanding of both substance abuse and family therapy was profoundly influenced by those years. I am particularly indebted to the influence of Dr. Genevra Zeigler-Driscoll, Marianne Walters, and Jay Haley, who were very important mentors to me during this period.

Since this book is not an academic text, it does not adequately document the many influences on my work from both the family therapy and substance abuse fields. I have been borrowing, integrating, and developing theoretical positions and treatment strategies for 20 years; at this point I do not know what to claim as uniquely mine. Although the ideas of many people helped shape my work, one person particularly influenced the development of my clinical thinking: David Berenson.

I met David in 1975, not long after his first seminal papers on family treatment of alcoholism were published. Since then my work has been profoundly influenced by his brilliant integration of alcoholism treatment and family therapy. I consider my work and that of many of my colleagues to be the fruit born from David Berenson's seeds. Thank you, David.

I would also like to thank Rich Simon, editor of the *Family Therapy Networker* who consistently returned my articles with cogent and tough comments and suggestions for more work. I am still not a very good writer, but I am indebted to Rich for helping me gain enough confidence to pursue this effort.

Susan Barrows, my editor at Norton, deserves special thanks for her gentle but firm management of my struggle to complete this book. Her careful attention to detail and search for clarity have been instrumental in helping many sections of this book transcend the author's tendencies to literary obfuscation.

I appreciate the tolerance of my clients, colleagues, and friends, many of whom have put up with the vagaries and impositions this book has created in my professional and private life. Special thanks to Faye Snider, who has been my teaching partner for the past ten years as well as a loyal supporter of this project, and my secretary, Grace Doyle, who manages the office with efficiency and good cheer and helps me get through each day.

1

The Family Album

In my office the family — parents Bob and Sally, sons John and Frank, and daughter Karen — showed me pictures. First there were the two families in which the parents had grown up. The faded pictures showed two rather formal-looking middle-class families. Dressed up for the photographer, they all stared at the camera and seemed to be saying cheese. The next set of photos began with the wedding pictures and included the baby pictures. Bob and Sally looked very young and very happy. There were a lot of pictures of the kids — Christmas, Little League, birthdays, and graduations. The pictures showed good times and good memories. While we flipped through the photos, they shared their stories.

*   *   *   *   *

There was silence at the table. Bobby's sisters stared at their plates and waited for Bobby to spill something or to say something dumb. Out of the corner of their eyes they watched their father eat and tried to figure out if it was going to be a bad night.

Bobby spat some gristle onto his plate. His father looked up and said harshly, "Don't spit at my table, Robert!"

"But, Dad, that was gristle," Bobby said defiantly.

"Don't talk back to me!"

"Leave me alone."

Usually Bobby got sent from the table. Sometimes his Dad smacked him. If it got out of hand, Mom would leave the table in tears. Sometimes his sister Ann would try and get them to stop, but more often the two little girls just sat in silence and waited for Bobby to take his licks and be sent to his room.

Later Jessica said to Ann, "Bobby's so dumb. I don't know why he's always picking fights with Dad."

*   *   *   *   *

Sally had a different relationship with her Dad. Even though he was a drinker, he never beat her or anything like that. He was always fun and lively; when he was drunk he didn't get obnoxious, just kind of silly. Sally remembers being his favorite. When she was little, he liked to tickle her. It would start off being fun and she would laugh, but then he wouldn't stop when she had had enough. She would get scared, but he would just laugh and hold her down. He tickled her tummy, her toes, and her armpits. He tickled her all over, even places where she knew he shouldn't be touching her. Even when she cried he wouldn't stop until *he* was done.

*   *   *   *   *

Sally's parents disapproved of Bob and Sally's marriage because they thought they were too young and that Bobby was too wild. But Sally loved riding on the back of his motorcycle and going to parties with him. He was always a lot of fun. Sally felt that she really understood Bobby and that underneath his tough guy act he was a very gentle boy. She was sure he would settle down after they got married. She also hoped that Bobby's need to have sex all the time would ease off a bit after they were able to be together all the time.

Bobby was so crazy about Sally that he never wanted to let her out of his sight. It surprised him when she agreed to marry him. He was determined to make her proud of him.

*   *   *   *   *

Bob really shaped up after marrying Sally. He went back to school and got his degree and landed a good job in a brokerage firm. Even though their sex life went straight downhill after the wedding, they managed quickly to produce two boys, first John and then, two years later, Frank. Loving the boys filled up their lives. After the boys went off to school, they couldn't resist having one more and were very pleased when it was a girl. They named her Karen.

Neither of them could remember exactly when Bob started having what he called "just one more little dose of warm Southern Comfort" after dinner.

* * * * *

Sally lay in bed pretending that she was asleep. She listened to Bob fumbling around in the bathroom. She heard him cursing under his breath because he couldn't find the tooth-paste. She knew he would come to bed soon. There wouldn't be any trouble because he knew better than to try anything if he had had too much to drink. He would just get into bed and fall asleep, reeking with the smell of cigarettes and alcohol. Then she would be able to go to sleep. She was very tired.

* * * * *

Bob, stuck in traffic, was very angry. He was thinking about his nonexistent sex life and what a cold fish Sally had turned into, wondering if he should tell her off once and for all. Suddenly somebody cut in front of him. He screamed out the window, "You sonofabitch! Look where you're going!" The close encounter left him rattled and even madder. He passed his favorite bar. "What the hell," he said to himself as he pulled into the parking lot. A voice in his head reminded him that he had promised himself that he would not stop for a drink on the way home. He knew she'd be mad but . . .

* * * * *

Bob liked being a Little League coach. He tried to be very patient with the boys because he remembered how obnoxious his own father had been when he was little. His father would come to the game drunk and then get loud and yell at the umpire. Bob was always careful not to do any drinking until after the game. He brought his cooler with him, but he didn't touch a can until the last out.

It really upset Bob when Frank quit the team in the middle of the season. There was just no excuse. Bob lost it that night like he never had before.

The next morning Bob woke up feeling sick. He didn't remember what happened the night before but he knew it had been bad. He knew he had gone after Frank. Then Sally had gotten into it. Had he hit her too? He wasn't sure. Then he remembered the blood. She had a bloody nose. He must have hit her. A rush of self-loathing, of nausea, swept over him.

He got up and made her some coffee. He wrote her a note and put it on the tray.

Dear Sally,

What happened last night was completely wrong. I don't know what happened to me but I know I can't lose my temper like that again. I never hit you before and I'll never do it again.

I love you,

Bobby

When Sally woke up her nose was swollen and there was some dried blood in her nostril. Bob brought her the coffee but she wouldn't speak to him. When she read the note she started to cry. Bob took her in her arms and she began to cry harder. He kept saying, "I'm sorry I'm sorry," over and over again as he held her.

After a while they began to have sex. It was awkward and hurried. Bob didn't last long. He apologized again and she told him that it was fine anyway.

Bob got dressed quickly. He called to her and said, "Listen, honey, let's make it a good day. Whatever you'd like me to do, you got it. I'm yours for the day. Okay, hon?"

Sally was still lying in bed. She didn't say anything. She didn't know what to say. She was worried about Frank and what to say to him. Her head was beginning to throb. She could feel a migraine coming on.

*   *   *   *   *

When Frank was a freshman in high school, he was suspended after being caught smoking pot in the boys' bathroom.
When Bob tried to talk to him, Frank wouldn't talk. Bob got
exasperated and gave Frank a good sound licking. Frank took it
in silence. His older brother, John, tried to give him some
advice about drugs, but Frank just scoffed at him, calling him
"a know-it-all."

When the school suggested that Frank get counseling, Bob
refused to have anything to do with it. Sally ended up taking
Frank a few times but it didn't get anywhere because Frank
wouldn't talk with the counselor.

*   *   *   *   *

The following year Sally was referred to a therapist by her
physician. When she was asked why she had come, she
responded:

I don't really know what I'm supposed to say. My doctor says that I
should see you because I get these migraines and I seem to be upset
a lot of the time. I don't really know why. I've got three great kids,
although I'm really worried about my middle son because he's been
getting in trouble a lot in school. My husband is basically a good
man. Sometimes we don't get along and sometimes we have fights
and that upsets me. But he tries hard and he's a pretty good father.
It's not like . . . I mean, sometimes he loses his temper but he's
never missed a day's work in his life and he doesn't run around on
me or anything like that. He says that I'm cold to him and I
suppose that's true. I'm just not interested in that kind of stuff
anymore. I don't know why. I don't know what's the matter with
me anyway. Frank worries me the most. He's just so angry and he
won't listen to anybody.

Sally did not stay in therapy very long because she found that
she didn't know what the therapist wanted her to do. She just
went and talked and he hardly said anything at all. She also
found that this talking made her very anxious.

*   *   *   *   *

After the boys went off to college, Karen had a bad time at
home and went through a period of crash dieting that

had greatly concerned Sally and Bob. They worked together to try to convince Karen to eat. Bob was very patient with her and even agreed to go with Sally to a counselor. They met a few times. Even though Karen talked very little, she did promise not to lose any more weight. The therapist tried to get them to talk about other issues but there wasn't much interest. After several sessions the problem seemed to get a little better and they stopped therapy.

*   *   *   *   *

Soon after this Bob was referred to an EAP counselor by his supervisor because he was getting into a lot of conflict with his colleagues. He went for a couple of sessions and was quite cooperative. He explained to the counselor that there was a lot of tension at home and that he was sure that he could get back on track at work. He was much more careful after that.

*   *   *   *   *

John, the older boy, decided to become a psychologist and went off to graduate school. Frank continued to be the center of the family's worries. He dropped out of college and took off on a motorcycle tour of the west coast. He came back with a cute girl named Annie. He was desperately in love with her. They couldn't wait to get married. At the wedding, Sally cried and cried. John drove his Dad home from the reception early because Bob had had too much to drink.

*   *   *   *   *

RECOGNIZING PATTERNS

Where does the cycle begin? It is not only alcoholism that is passed down from one generation to the next, but also the pattern of behavior and interaction that surrounds alcoholism in families. Growing up in their respective families, Bob and Sally have been well trained for the roles they play out in their marriage. Bob's dependence on alcohol evolves in small increments, enabling the family slowly to adjust to the drinking, as Bob adjusts to the family. Bob's use of alcohol allows Sally to avoid intimacy, while

Sally's distance allows Bob to justify turning to a drink. The more Bob drinks the more he becomes an outsider in the family, until eventually he is more a problem to be managed than a family member.

As the parents adapt, so do the children. John becomes an assistant parent and tries to keep the family working together. In so doing he further usurps Dad's position. Frank becomes the lightning rod for all the family tensions, absorbing most of the anger and worry. This distracts the other family members from the impasse of Sally and Bob's relationship and Bob's increasingly troublesome drinking. When the older boys leave home, Karen takes a turn at having a problem that distracts Mom and Dad.

Over time the whole family learns how to live with alcoholism and play out the typical pattern of interactions that surround and maintain it. For Bob and Sally, this family is not so different from their families of origin. Only their positions have changed. It feels oddly normal to them, just as the enduring dark and cold of the Arctic winter is normal to Eskimos.

Over the course of Bob and Sally's marriage, the family has several contacts with the mental health system. Frank is brought to treatment for being suspended from school. Sally presents her migraines and depression. Karen sees someone around her weight issues. Bob is referred because of his conflicts at work. Yet the pattern of alcohol abuse is never addressed and the family as a whole is never treated. Bob and Sally do not ask for help. Do Eskimos complain about the cold?

A large proportion of all clients in the mental health system, regardless of the nature of the presenting problem, comes from alcoholic and/or highly dysfunctional family systems. Yet clients seldom mention drinking problems in their parents or grandparents. Many clinicians perceive this avoidance of the alcohol issue as a form of resistance; for these clients and their families, however, it is a form of survival. Acknowledging the drinking would threaten the life of the family; once the issue was finally out in the open, the family could never return to the status quo.

If Bob's drinking had been challenged, would the family have been able to remain intact? There is a good chance that Bob would not have stopped drinking and that the couple would have been faced with the stark choice of living with an irreconcilable difference or of divorcing. This would have been particularly true if Bob's drinking were still in the relatively early stages of development, when it would be easy for him to continue to deny the problem. It is also true that all marriages are built around a series of acknowledged and covert compromises. Both Bob and Sally know each other's vulnerabilities; essentially they have agreed to a covert mutual protection pact ("I won't confront you if you don't confront me").

Frank, the son, would know better than to tell the counselor about Dad's drinking and his occasional violence, because he was aware of what would happen to him if his father ever found out. Karen, with her father sitting right in front of her, would have found it even harder to mention the drinking during therapy sessions. Bob was certainly not going to bring up the drinking to his EAP counselor because he was afraid that it might cost him his job. Is it any wonder that families will present to the mental health system an acting-out child, a psychosomatic symptom, or a marital conflict rather than talking about drinking? The conspiracy of silence is safer.

As clinicians, we sometimes collude inadvertently with the family system to avoid the issue of substance abuse by not looking for it, not knowing how to work with it when we find it, or pushing too hard at it. When obviously destructive to the individual and the life of the family, substance abuse is hard to treat but not hard to see. When addiction is clearly identified, most clinicians, regardless of orientation, will shift the focus of treatment to the chemical dependency, refer to such self-help groups as AA and Al-Anon, and encourage abstinence. Treating substance abuse is significantly more difficult when abusers are in the earlier stages of the problem and there has been little obvious impairment in their lives. Many abusers are able to work effectively, maintain social and family relationships, and limit their use of chemicals to evenings and weekends. It may be very difficult for them, their families, and the therapist to see that it is their chemical dependency that is having a corrosive effect on their personality and their relationships with the people closest to them. It then becomes doubly difficult for clinicians to address the drinking issue, since neither the drinker nor other family members are likely to bring up the drinking, much less see it as a central problem that needs to be addressed.

As therapists, we have tended to fall into three distinct categories in our responses to early stages of substance abuse in families, depending on whether we are psychodynamically oriented individual therapists, family therapists, or chemical dependency specialists.

Individual psychodynamically oriented therapists tend not to see the abusing member of a family system because the abuser is rarely the one seeking treatment. More often than not the patient is a spouse or a child of an abuser or an adult who grew up with an alcoholic parent. The therapy is oriented primarily toward helping the client work through his or her own issues rather than engaging the larger system and possibly exposing the substance abuse problem. It is often the case that the substance abuse is never even mentioned in the course of individual treatment.

If the abuser himself is in psychodynamic psychotherapy and is a successful, well-functioning adult, then he is likely to be minimizing or avoiding entirely his dependence on chemicals. One man I treated had spent eight years in analysis without ever mentioning to his analyst that he was drinking almost a fifth of whiskey every night after he got home from work. Since the therapist is working with the client individually, he may never have access to the true state of the dependency; he will not hear from other members of the family about his outrageous behavior while drinking, and he will not get an accurate picture from the client.

While family therapists do have access to the family, substance abuse is frequently not part of the presenting problem. Either the abuser will not come to therapy (the father who can never get time off from work) or no one in the family will mention that there is a problem at home. Even when abuse is identified, many family therapists tend to assume that, if the abuser is still basically functioning well, then it's possible to treat the chemical dependency as a symptom of the family dynamics. If the family system changes, then maybe the abuse problem will resolve itself. For example, it is fairly common for family therapists to attempt to empower the peripheral parent (usually the father) as a first step in therapy. If Dad has a moderate drinking problem, the therapist may assume that, as Dad becomes more effective in his role as father and husband, his need to use alcohol will dissipate. Sometimes this approach has positive short-term effects; however, it has been my experience that, if the role of the substance abuse is not addressed, then the gains made in the therapy do not last and the old pattern reemerges.

Both individual and family therapists tend to get into trouble by either not recognizing the substance abuse problem or not knowing how to confront it directly. For the chemical dependency specialist, the problem is often the opposite. Counselors who deal with serious addiction most of the time, may focus much too quickly on the drinking as the main issue, regardless of the presenting problem. They may believe that nothing can be done with either the individual or the family until the substance abuse problem is addressed and the client accepts the need to go to AA and practice abstinence. This position oftentimes leads to massive resistance, denial, and ultimately a stuck case.

WORKING ASSUMPTIONS

I have been working with families like Bob and Sally's for many years and yet I still find it difficult to navigate my way through one of these cases. Should I work with the presenting problem and deal with the drinking indirectly, or do I need to focus on the alcohol issue even at the risk of losing the case? How hard should I try to see all the members of the family if they are resistant to that idea? Should I be using the "disease model" of alcoholism and pushing for AA and abstinence, or should I be helping the client learn to drink appropriately? When does therapy become potentially part of the enabling and denial system rather than part of the solution? These questions always arise, but answering them is never easy. Case by case, the answers are always a little different.

In order to do celestial navigation, you have to start with what is called an "assumed position" representing your approximation of where you are. This is then compared to the actual sextant reading of the angle of the sun, enabling you to calculate your real position. In working with substance abusing families, I begin with a series of assumptions about how substance abuse and family systems interact; these assumptions are then compared to each family's unique patterns and characteristics. Following are some of the "assumed positions" that I use to help me keep track of where I am and to provide a reference point for assessing each family.

A Working Definition of Substance Abuse

Defining substance abuse is like being an art critic. It is all in the eye of the beholder. Much progress has been made toward defining alcoholism and drug addiction, both as physical and psychological processes; however, defining substance abuse requires much more subtlety, since the range of possible ways of understanding it is much broader. Thus, there is a much greater likelihood of subjectivity and arbitrariness. Throughout this book I will be discussing interventions with families in which substance abuse is in its earliest stages, often long before there is any clear-cut possibility of labeling the abuse as either alcoholism or drug addiction. Consequently, it behooves me to give my own subjective working definition of substance abuse.

Substance abuse exists when an individual has a pattern of being dependent on the use of substances (i.e., alcohol and prescribed or illegal drugs) to alter and control mood states, is unable to easily regulate this use, and experiences some form of distress if unexpectedly deprived of access to it. Substance abuse is clearly the precurser to alcoholism and addiction; however, those who abuse chemicals will not necessarily become addicted or be unable to learn how to use substances appropriately.

Clearly this description is very inclusive. I think substance abuse can and does exist long before one sees obvious loss of control or the onset of overt physical, psychological, or interpersonal symptoms. While alcoholics and drug addicts cannot regulate or predict either the frequency or the amount of their use of chemicals, substance abusers frequently can and do control their dependency on chemicals, albeit with considerable effort. For instance, Bob never drank during Little League games, but he never came to games without his cooler either. This control allows the substance abuser a very subtle form of denial about his relationship to the chemical.

Using an inclusive definition is important for at least a couple of reasons. First, substance abuse is frequently missed by clinicians in its earliest stages, when neither the individual nor the family is able to see or acknowledge any overt signs of the potential problem.

Unless the therapist is looking for it, he or she is likely to miss it as well. Secondly, in the early stages many substance-abusing clients can be treated successfully without the therapist's having to push AA and abstinence as the only solution. On the other hand, many substance abusers seem clearly to be on the road to addiction; early detection and treatment may allow them to abstain and use AA without the enormously high cost of hitting bottom.

The Three-Generational Perspective

To the outsider, what is most incomprehensible about the substance-abusing family system is that, even when the pattern has advanced to the level of profound dysfunction, often including physical and sexual abuse, the family will resist change and continue to cover up, enable, and deny the substance abuse as an issue. In order to understand the stability of these systems, it is useful to maintain a three-generational perspective. Adults who as children were trapped inside alcoholic or seriously dysfunctional families clearly are the most prone to repeat the pattern due to both inheritance and learned behavior. Understanding how people tolerate and inadvertently perpetuate their own or their spouses' substance abuse begins with understanding their experience of growing up as kids in substance-abusing families and how living with the pattern of substance abuse became normal.

To grow up in alcoholic family is to be shaped by an environment in which the people we are most dependent upon behave in a very inconsistent and destructive manner. How does a little girl deal with the confusion of feeling the uncomfortable yet pleasing experience of being "tickled" by her father? How does a boy integrate the experience of being beaten by his father for no particular offense and then blamed by his mother and his siblings "for making trouble"?

Children survive growing up in alcoholic systems by learning to distrust others, becoming self-sufficient, blocking out their feelings, and becoming rigidly attached to roles that give them a sense of their place and identity within the family. One of the most successful survival skills for children from such families is to learn how to ignore what is going on at home and to repress any feelings about it. These children are trapped in scary situations they cannot understand, control, or escape. They have no choice. They learn how to subsist on very little parental constancy and support. Like the poor kid who stands longingly in front of the toy store window and then walks away muttering, "I didn't want that dumb old toy anyway," these children generally give up their expectations of both parents. They feel that they don't deserve any better. They may fantasize about how it will be different when they grow up, but they secretly assume that things will always be the same. They are well trained to take abuse and live with chaos.

Those who have brought to popular attention the Adult Children of Alcoholics phenomenon — people like Sharon Wegscheider-Cruse, Claudia Black, Robert Ackerman, and Janet Woititz — have discussed how such children tend to develop rigid roles to help them cope. The most common of these family roles are the hero, the scapegoat, and the lost child.

The *hero* is usually the oldest child. Like John, the future psychologist, this child assumes the position of the assistant parent taking on a large measure of responsibility for the younger siblings as well as serving as a parent's confidant and helpmate. The child's sense of identity and self-esteem often become quite dependent on being a competent caretaker whose experience of intimacy and relatedness is derived from an ability to give to others. As an adult this child stands a reasonably good chance of marrying a dysfunctional spouse or becoming a caretaker or a workaholic.

The *scapegoat* serves as a lightning rod for family tension and conflict. By routing tension through this child, the family is able to avoid a confrontation around the drinking issue, which might threaten the family status quo. The acting-out kid protects Dad from being confronted, protects Mom from having to challenge Dad, protects his siblings from getting the heat, and ultimately protects himself from the anxiety of being passive and waiting for the next crisis. Since scapegoats act out, they are frequently brought in for treatment and therefore are usually the first family member to get help. If they are not helped, the likelihood that they will become alcoholic or drug dependent is quite high. Bobby was the scapegoat in his family and his son, Frank filled the same role in the next generation.

The *lost child* develops the skill of being unobtrusive and detached. Usually one of the younger children, this child intuitively recognizes that the best method of staying out of harm's way is to make oneself scarce. These children frequently avoid being home as much as possible and often turn to other adults and surrogate families for support and closeness. As adults, these children tend to remain very peripheral and detached and may be unable to develop close relationships. They are also prone to turn to chemicals as a way of relieving their isolation and overcoming their inhibitions.

Needless to say, the scarring of children is not unique to the substance-abusing family. All the tendencies described above also emerge in families in which there is a chronically ill or insane parent, an early death of a parent, incest or physical abuse, or a particularly destructive divorce. Whether in an alcoholic or a dysfunctional system, children develop a rigid set of defenses that are held onto at all costs. Thus, caretakers are just as dependent on their role as scapegoats may be dependent on chemicals. When these children grow up, their early survival strategies can become major stumbling blocks in adult relationships, since they cannot tolerate the vulnerability of giving up their safe position. It is not surprising that, having grown up learning how to tolerate the intolerable, deny the obvious, and blame themselves for the destructive behavior of others, they are prone to become abusers, marry one, or be the parent of one. The role you know is safer than any role you don't. Caretakers marry scapegoats and the cycle continues. Is it any wonder that these couples "resist" therapeutic entreaties to change? They truly don't know any better.

The Coevolutionary System

When did Bob cross over the line into substance abuse? Did the family and couple dynamics cause the drinking? Or did the drinking cause the family dynamics? The abuse of chemicals by a family member helps to regulate how individuals experience and express feelings, how spouses maintain a balance of closeness and distance as well as their particular hierarchial positions. Through an infinite series of small adjustments family members learn to cope with an abusing member. As they adapt to him he adapts to them. The pattern is supported by the internal restraints of the abuser, which allow him to maintain a high enough level of functioning so that the family and social systems to which he belongs do not reject him. The pattern is also sustained by the family's responses. Regardless of whether family members are actively fighting the problem or putting their heads in the sand and denying it, their willingness to coexist with the user sustains the pattern of the substance abuse.

Given this "chicken and egg" situation, I assume that substance abuse and the family's pattern of behavior surrounding it are coevolutionary. This approach frees the therapist from a theory of causality that might overly determine treatment priorities. For example, in the case of Bob and Sally, if I assume that Bob's drinking is the root cause of all the family's problems, then I may feel obligated to push the disease model of alcoholism and prescribe AA and abstinence long before he or the family is ready. It is essential that I work with both the drinker's and family's perceptions around the appropriate use of alcohol and help them discover whether by their own criteria they are able to manage their use of alcohol appropriately. It is far better for the family and the drinker to confront the issue than for me to attempt to provide the necessary motivation.

Appreciating the coevolutionary nature of the system leads one to see the family's enabling and denial behavior as adaptive and protective of the stability of the whole system. Just as it is important to avoid being precipitous in confronting the drinking behavior, it is essential for me to maintain a nonjudgmental and empathic response to the family members' inadvertent part in perpetuating the drinking. Family members are just as dependent on their roles as abusers are on chemicals. Nevertherless, there are times when even those of us who have developed considerable understanding and empathy for alcoholics and their disease will find ourselves becoming somewhat impatient with family members who cannot break out of the cycle of enabling and denial.

Substance Abusing Systems Eventually Become Destabilized

Although it is clear that these family systems develop a considerable degree of stability, eventually they begin to break down and thus become accessible for treatment. There are several reasons why the substance abuse pattern becomes destabilized.

Situational. There may be an external situation, such as the loss of a job, illness of a family member, or family relocation, that creates an overload of stress. Families will often respond to these stresses by exacerbating their already established pattern of handling difficulties through reliance on chemicals. For a family that is managing a certain degree of abuse under "normal" circumstances, there is very little margin for error when bad times hit and the user seeks solace in the bottle. When the husband loses his job, his routine six beers a night, which the family had learned to tolerate, can easily evolve into a case a day, as he tries to manage his loss of self-esteem and the dramatic increase of time on his hands. A controlled pattern of alcohol abuse may become out-of-control alcoholic drinking. Yet the family's response is often to maintain the same level of enabling behavior and denial, even though the substance abuse has clearly become much worse and is no longer adaptive for anyone. Conversely, family members may begin to argue about the substance abuse as a distraction from their anxiety about the job loss and their resulting economic crisis. Fighting for his manly right to drink on his own terms may be the husband's way of maintaining his sense of self-worth and power in the face of this external loss of status. Criticizing his drinking may be his wife's indirect way of expressing her displeasure at him for losing his job (without blaming him directly).

Developmental transitions. Transitions in the family life cycle that cause stress for all families will frequently destabilize a normal pattern of abuse. A wife may find that her tolerance for her husband's drinking changes dramatically after she has a child. She might become more concerned about his drinking and driving or the possibility of his having too much to drink and not being able to respond to the child in an emergency. Conversely a husband's drinking, which may have been covertly limited by his wife's monitoring, may escalate if the wife shifts the primary focus of her attention to their newborn child and away from him.

The children's reaching adulthood and readiness to leave home may well create another major developmental crisis for the family. At this critical juncture in the life of the family, the husband and wife have to renegotiate their relationship from one that is primarily focused on being parents to one that revolves around their being a couple. This tends to affect their pattern of managing closeness and distance in their couple relationship. If historically she relied on the children to meet many of her emotional needs and he maintained his distance through his work, then she may turn to the comfort of alcohol as she struggles to compensate for the loss of her children. As the spouses begin to struggle over the abuse, it becomes a substitute for their underlying conflicts around intimacy and takes the place of the children as the focal point of their lives.

Any of the major transitions in the family life cycle will cause considerable distress and call for realignment in the family system. The family that has already accommodated to a pattern of substance abuse is likely to get into serious trouble during these periods. It is as if the family members were teetering at the edge of the cliff and the transitional crisis strikes and gives them a final push.

Progressive disease processes. The family's ability to tolerate the substance abuse often destabilizes because of the progressive evolution of substance abuse into alcoholism or addiction. Regardless of whether the chemical is cocaine, alcohol, pot, or prescription drugs, a significant proportion of the users will become unable to control their use and the consequent personality and behavioral changes. Clearly many users for physiological and psychological reasons cannot remain in the intermediate stage of chemical dependency that we are calling substance abuse. They move relatively quickly from use to abuse to addiction, regardless of the impact of their behavior on their relationships and the negative responses of others.

While many substance abusers maintain some control over their dependency because of their own internal restraints and because of the regulatory responses of their family and social network, many others cannot regulate themselves and their family's responses reinforce the increasing addiction. In these case the family's ability to tolerate the substance abuse begins to break down as the abuser becomes progressively more out of control.

It is usually when the system is in its earliest stages of destabilization that individuals within the family become symptomatic and ask for help from the outside world. Rarely is the substance abuse the original symptom presented for treatment. Any one of the family members may be the symptom bearer. The overresponsible

wife may develop psychosomatic symptoms like Sally's migraines.
The parental child may have psychosomatic symptoms or an eating
disorder. The scapegoat will most likely get in trouble with acting
out behavior or his own substance abuse. The younger children
may be noticed by their schools for learning disabilities, withdrawn social behaviors, or even too much clowning around, depending on their role in the family. The substance abuser may be
referred for treatment for health or job-related reasons without the
alcohol being part of the presenting problem.

The Dual Function of the Presenting Problem

I think of the original presenting problem as having two potentially quite contradictory functions in the life of the family. Whether the problem is a child, a marriage, or a specific symptom, it can
be understood as the family's coping system beginning to show
signs of breaking down and a way in which the family crosses its
own boundaries to seek help in the outside world; on the other
hand, the organization of the family around a symptom bearer can
also be seen as the way that the family stabilizes itself and detours a
family breakdown. Thus, the symptom can be both a plea for help
and a shield that protects the family from having to address the
drinking directly. Four times members of Bob and Sally's family
were referred for treatment; yet each time the family managed to
avoid having to confront the issues around Bob's drinking. When
substance abuse itself is the presenting problem, it also serves a
dual purpose, representing both a reaching out for help and a
distraction from other hard-to-address family issues. That the
struggle around the drinking can operate as a distraction and be
protective of the family becomes more obvious when one observes
family members going through the intense difficulty of learning
how to relate to one another after the drinker is no longer using
alcohol.

It is important to realize that the presenting symptom represents
both a hand reaching out for help and a defensive wall behind
which the family can retreat, because the key to working with this
population is being able to engage the family around the presenting problem while assessing when and how to shift to the substance abuse issues in the system. Conversely, if the drinking is the

presenting symptom and it is effectively treated, the family members will need help as they work through the anxiety and confusion that ensue after they are no longer being organized and protected by the drinking pattern.

These "assumed positions" give me a starting point from which to think about where a given family is in relationship to substance abuse and how I as the therapist can engage the family. However, getting an accurate fix on each family begins with the knowledge that the family is always in a somewhat different place from where I think it is.

The treatment models I use in working with substance-abusing families are all based on beginning treatment around the the presenting problem. While they provide ways of organizing therapy, they cannot be followed blindly. Many sailors use chart kits which have sailing courses already plotted out on the charts as a way of orgainzing their passages. These preplanned course kits always contain a warning to the reader. It seems appropriate to include it here: Magnetic tracks between navigation aids and landmarks are given for planning purposes only and should not be relied on for other purposes.

*   *   *   *   *

By the time Bob and Sally came into treatment with me, Bob was a full-blown alcoholic ripe for sobriety. He had lost his job, he had had his license revoked for driving under the influence, and his health was shot. Also, John had confronted Sally about her denial until she finally decided to go to Al-Anon.

Bob went into inpatient treatment on the day after his 56th birthday. As Sally looked at him lying in the bed in his hospital johnny with his hair mussed up and a frightened look in his eyes, she thought to herself, "He looks like an old man."

*   *   *   *   *

A couple of years after Bob got sober, I began to work with the whole family around issues of coming to terms with the past. We had the meeting where Sally, Bob, John, Frank, and Karen went through photo albums together, looked at the pictures, and acknowledged the painful struggle they had gone through. There were several moments of shared grief and shared anger for all the wasted years. There was some surprise at how happy they all seemed to appear in the pictures and some recognition that there were good times as well as bad. There was also the aching wish that somehow they should have been able to get help sooner, that the story didn't have to come out this way. At one point, Frank came across a picture of his father when Bob was about six. The little boy in the picture had a tense angry grimace on his face.

"Why did you look so angry, Dad?" Frank asked lightly.

Tears filled Bob's eyes but he fought to hold them back. He looked out the window and said quietly to no one in particular, "I don't know what happened. I hated my old man. And look at me. Forty years go by and I end up a drunk just like him. I can't believe it went on for so long. I can't believe I didn't do anything about it. I guess I'm nothing but a chip off the old block."

Tears slid down Bob's cheeks as he looked away. Sally began to cry. I felt the tears come to my eyes. I wanted to give him a hug, but I was afraid to let myself. I wasn't sure who needed the hug. I was suddenly thinking of my mother and all the years she saw doctors and never got help. I wanted to say something healing, but I couldn't think of anything. After a few minutes of silence Frank said, "Well, Dad, at least you're a sober chip."

*   *   *   *   *

Bob did not get sober until he hit bottom and his kids were grown-up. Can families like this one be helped earlier? I think so. This book is about breaking the cycle before it's too late. It is about how we can work with Bob and Sally and their kids when they make their first contact with us, when they know that something is wrong but cannot tell us, when they want help but are afraid to change.

2

Storm Preparations: Couples Therapy, Part One

PRESENTING PROBLEMS

Joan would get stoned every night just before Hank came home from work. Hank always wanted to talk about his day. When Joan was stoned, his talking didn't bother her any more than the incessant clacking of the cicadas in their backyard.

Hank initiated couples therapy because he felt that they had a communication problem.

*　　*　　*　　*　　*

Ann says the problem is Arthur's drinking. Arthur tells her that it is her fault because she nags all the time — and furthermore, he doesn't really have a drinking problem. He says that she just picks on him because her father was an alcoholic and she's obsessed about drinking. He claims she's the one who needs the help.

Ann seeks individual therapy in order to figure out whether or not she is too sensitive to Arthur's drinking.

*　　*　　*　　*　　*

They both know that he's an alcoholic. Eileen goes to Al-Anon and Martin goes occasionally to AA. Martin is still actively drinking, though he has periods of abstinence. After a binge, he is very apologetic and acknowledges openly that his drinking causes all their problems.

They want couples therapy so that he will stop drinking.

*   *   *   *   *

Sally's doctor is worried about her headaches. The doctor doesn't know about Bob's drinking and the marital problems. He sends her to therapy for help in dealing with stress that might contribute to her migraines.

When Sally goes to the therapist she isn't entirely sure why she is there.

*   *   *   *   *

As these individuals and couples appear in my office, I am often reminded of being at sea and watching the barometer drop. I know a storm is coming. I can see the portents in the sky. I pretend to myself that I am calm as I go about my preparations. It feels better to be preparing. It provides the illusion of control.

Substance-abusing systems generally don't change without a major crisis. It is my job to set up the crisis in the family or couple so that it results in people's being able to confront the abuse and go into recovery. However, even with thorough preparations crises are no more controllable than storms at sea. You just prepare as best you can. Then you wait and hope.

Couples present for treatment in a myriad of different ways. Yet all of these couples are still in the active phase of the substance abuse cycle, with one or both members of the system using and abusing chemicals. Some couples know that there is a significant substance abuse problem but present some other issue to the therapist. Others are simply unaware of the impact of the substance abuse. Still others are engaged in an active tug of war about the substance abuse issue. Some spouses come in for individual treatment; others come in as couples, but convinced that one member has all the problems.

There are essentially two kinds of presenting problems within a couple system. First, there are couples organized around a symptom in one member. The marriage is not the focus of treatment; rather, the individual is seen as the problem and may be the only one seeking treatment. Symptoms such as agoraphobia, depression, psychosomatic complaints, and even alcoholism typify these couples. The couple system is organized in a way that allows one member to be the strong one or caretaker and the other to be the dependent or sick one. The symptomatic problem tends to enable the couple to maintain a certain functional, mutually protective status quo. In the case of Sally and her migraines, her treatment does not threaten either her marriage or the unity of her family. Bob can be a supportive spouse and Sally can get help; neither will have to deal with the risk of exposing their marital tensions and his drinking problem. The symptom allows the marital struggle to remain covert, unresolved, and stable.

Other couples may be in a struggle around substance, but present problems in their marital relationship for treatment. For instance, consider the case of Joan and Hank, where clearly Joan is dependent on marijuana but the couple presents "communication problems" to the therapist. The symmetrical struggle between the spouses is often a mechanism that protects one or both from having to resolve their own individual developmental issues. The "communication problem" is safer for Joan and Hank than her drug abuse or his deep sense of insecurity.

This treatment model is designed for couples with a pattern of substance abuse, regardless of whether it is part of the presenting problem, undisclosed by either member of the couple, or altogether hidden, as in the case where one member of the couple seeks treatment for an entirely different symptom.

MAKING THE TRANSITION FROM INDIVIDUAL TO COUPLES THERAPY

Before I discuss the six-stage couples treatment model, let me turn to the particular issue of how to respond to an individual's request for treatment when he or she is part of a marital or committed couple system. For three reasons I try to engage the couple in treatment right from the beginning of therapy, even though only one individual may be seeking help.

First, if there is unacknowledged substance abuse, then it is important to see the couple in order to assess the possibility of abuse and the pattern of behavior that may maintain it. In Sally and Bob's case, Sally was referred to treatment for her migraines. She was not ready to risk focusing on her husband's drinking, partly due to lack of awareness and partly due to unconscious fear. If Bob had been part of the treatment from the beginning, the therapist would have observed their pattern of interactions and might have detected his alcohol abuse. While clients can easily avoid issues they are uncomfortable addressing, their behavior pattern reveals these underlying issues in much the same way a fingerprint betrays a unique identity. Seeing how spouses work together clearly provides the therapist with a level of information different from one person's point of view. Some therapists are very skilled at seeing individuals and extrapolating a contextual perspective that allows them to work effectively. I find this to be quite difficult. I need to see how the parts of the engine work together before I can begin to fix the "broken" part.

Secondly, it is very difficult to intiate couples treatment effectively after you have begun therapy with one member of the couple. The natural process of developing an alliance with the client creates an imbalance in the couple system when the therapist attempts to incorporate the spouse at a later date. For example, if Sally had entered treatment for her migraines and after a while the focus of her problems had shifted to her marital relationship and Bob's drinking, it would have been almost impossible to engage Bob in a nonthreatening manner. Sally and the therapist would be in a collusive relationship, in which they had discussed issues that Sally had not broached with Bob. Regardless of how carefully the therapist attempted to approach him at this point, Bob would feel ganged up on by the therapist and his own wife, this pair who share secrets that exclude him.

Seeing the partners together from the beginning helps me gauge the risks of change for both of them and to maximize the possibility that they will be able to change and grow together. If I do see an individual because I cannot engage the spouse, as in the case of Ann and Arthur, then I proceed with the individual work and, when the time comes for couples treatment, I refer the couple to another therapist.

My third reason for always working with couples is that it is too easy for me to fall into the role of the overfunctioning, overresponsible spouse when the substance abuser comes in alone. The spouse at home may continue to engage in enabling behavior that props up the substance abuser, while in my one hour a week I am trying to create change. Not only am I likely to be in a tug of war with my client, but I may also be undermined by the spouse. The therapy evolves into a game: I slip into trying to monitor the substance abuse and the client dissembles and manipulates so he or she won't get caught. If I work with the couple, then the abuser's games and the spouse's enabling behavior can be simultaneously addressed. The game becomes a problem between them; they carry the responsibility for either changing or accepting it. If I work with the abuser alone, then the problem is between him/her and me. Some therapists are superb at dealing with abusers one on one. I am terrible at it. Frequently when I end an individual session, the client feels fine and I am exhausted from working so hard.

It is easy to say that it's a good idea for therapists to engage the couple when one member is the presenting problem. However, it is not always easy to get both spouses to the office. This is particularly true when neither spouse is asking for couples therapy. If one assumes that the symptom bearer serves a protective function for the couple by offering him/herself to the outside world as the problem, then it is important to accept the system on these terms, even when you are organizing the case somewhat differently. I follow three strategies in engaging both spouses.

(1) I accept the validity of the individual's desire to work on a particular problem and invite the spouse to participate as a concerned and potentially helpful supporter. If there is some resistance to this idea, then I negotiate a one-session consultation with both spouses. I explain that this consultation will enhance my understanding of the symptom by allowing me to hear how each partner describes the problem and how they as a couple have dealt with it. It is usually difficult for the spouse to refuse to come to a session couched as a one-time meeting. The process of negotiating this involvement uncovers considerable information about the marital system and its relationship to the presenting problem.

(2) In the interview itself, I avoid marital issues, even though they may be very evident. I organize the consultation around track-

ing the presenting problem and developing strategies for the symptom bearer to manage the symptoms more effectively and for the spouse to take part as a supportive helper. For example, if Sally and Bob came in because of Sally's migraines, I would inquire about the pattern of headaches, asking about various family members' responses and particular responses that are perceived to be helpful or unhelpful. While beginning to engage the couple, I would stay within the metaphor of Sally's having the problem.

(3) At the end of the session, I give homework assignments that engage both of them in the continuation of the treatment and maintain the spouse in a significant role as a supporter of the symptom bearer. This step allows me to keep the couple engaged in treatment while setting up a contract that is initially safe for both of them. For example, I might have given Bob and Sally the job of noticing if there was any discernible pattern to the frequency and duration of her headaches. My hope is that they will both come to the next session to compare notes.

These three steps allow me to engage the couple even though the request is for individual therapy; in addition, they provide the opportunity to see and ultimately address the other issues in the system, including hidden substance abuse. Once I have made the therapeutic environment safe and supportive for both partners, then opening up other issues in the system becomes less difficult.

If I had been Bob and Sally's therapist when she had her migraines, I probably would have spent several sessions on her headaches, a few sessions on coparenting, and a few sessions on marital stress. Then, finally, we would have been able to move to the issues around substance abuse.

Pacing the treatment so that clients can feel safe and supported enough to risk change is complicated and challenging. Confronting Bob and Sally about their marriage and his drinking early in the therapy would probably have precipitated their retreat from treatment. It takes patience and a sense of timing to know when to encourage the couple to go beyond the presenting problem to address the other issues in the system. I usually wait until there has been some real progress on resolving the presenting problem. Sometimes it is clear, however, that no progress can be made until the hidden issues are brought out in the open. My approach will obviously vary because each case is different.

Frequently I am concerned that my guess is wrong, that my

timing is off. Sometimes I push too quickly and sometimes I do not push hard enough. Fortunately, I have learned to backpedal when I have opened up material that the couple is unable to handle. If a couple recoils, then I refocus on safer issues. For example, if with Bob and Sally we were in the delicate transition where we were beginning to talk about the marriage and his drinking and I sensed their mutual discomfort and unreadiness, I would revert to the subject of Sally's migraines rather than continue to push. This shift back to a safer topic may enable them to bring up hard issues without feeling overwhelmed by them. If I take a leadership role in retreating from an issue broached prematurely then they will have less need to regress or withdraw in order to protect themselves from me. My hope is that the next time we touch the issue, it will be just a little easier for the couple to talk about it. This slow and deliberate process of opening up and closing over issues allows me to engage the couple safely.

Some couples simply resolve the presenting problem and avoid dealing with other issues, at least for the time being. For others the original symptom is a springboard from which they dive into their whole relationship. I try to remember that ultimately how far they go is their choice, not mine. My job as therapist/architect is to provide some possible blueprints; their job is to pick the house they want and then build it.

ASSESSING SUBSTANCE ABUSE IN THE COUPLE SYSTEM

Most couples I see have already chosen couples counseling, and so I do not have to go through the delicate preliminaries described above to engage them. Nevertheless it often happens that substance abuse is not mentioned as part of the presenting problem, although the behavior pattern suggests that one exists. In order to effectively address unacknowledged abuse, I need to first develop a good working relationship with the spouses and then raise the issue in a way that does not threaten them too much.

*   *   *   *   *

I was nervous. I had spent the morning telling an audience about how to confront unacknowledged substance abuse problems. I had made it sound so simple. Now I was going to do a demonstration interview with a couple. My stomach was tight. As I waited for the couple, along with the audience, I began making bad jokes about locking myself in the men's room.

Frank and Sue both looked scared. He sat with his arms folded across his chest and she hunched over in her chair with her knees pressed tightly together. She sat on her hands; her eyes flitted back and forth as she watched her husband, her therapist, and me. They knew that they were on tape and that people were watching on closed circuit TV. They were coming in for a consultation. After several months of therapy, they and their therapist felt that the treatment was at an impasse. The original presenting problem revolved around dealing with Frank's 17-year-old daughter from a previous marriage. They had not been able to get the daughter, who lived with them, to come to treatment. The therapist reported that as the case had evolved, Frank had complained about Sue's unwillingness to be sexual, and Sue, in turn, had complained about Frank's drinking. He had denied that there was any real drinking problem.

Both Frank and Sue lost their fathers at a young age. Both had destructive first marriages. They described their current relationship as the best that either of them had ever had. Neither of them really wanted to talk about Frank's drinking. Neither did I. After I had been in the room with them for five minutes, I could feel their anxiety and their unspoken wish not to be pushed toward an issue they were unprepared to confront. My dilemma was that I wanted to open up and assess the drinking issue without seeming to join with Sue against Frank, which would elicit considerable defensiveness on his part.

Throughout this chapter I will be using the transcript from my session with Frank and Sue to illustrate some of the ways that I engage a couple around substance abuse issues. While the interview provides some good examples, the reader needs to be forewarned that this is not a typical session. I was entering the case as the highly empowered consultant. Thus, I was able to accomplish more in one session than would have been possible if I had been seeing the couple for the first time in my office. Ironically, therapy is almost always easier in these demonstration interviews because the clients are on their best behavior. Knowing this should make me less nervous, but it never does.

Below I discuss several ways of engaging a couple and opening up the question of possible substance abuse in a nonthreatening and nonjudgmental fashion.

Joining the Couple System

Before I even consider raising issues about possible substance abuse, I must develop a relationship with a couple and begin to get to know the spouses' strengths and successes. Rather than begin with an immediate discussion of their problems, I take some time to get to know them as people and to inquire about what they do well. It is is easy to forget how threatening therapy can be for most people. Taking the time to engage people around their positive qualities helps to establish a respectful relationship. Often I ask spouses: What do you like best about your relationship? What do you like about each other? What is your greatest area of success as a couple? As individuals? I want to establish right from the beginning that therapy is a matter of identifying and enhancing clients' strengths, rather than exposing their weaknesses. They are partners in the process, not patients to be passively "treated."

D.T.   So it sounds like one of the things that you guys do best is really talk about things.

SUE   I think that's right. My first husband and I never talked about anything. Everything turned into a big fight.

FRANK   I gotta agree with Sue. Right from the start we always said that we have to tell each other everything.

D.T.   It sounds like that's an important strength that you have that really will come in handy when you're going through tough times. A lot of couples don't talk about the hard stuff.

The next joining procedure is simply using matching techniques to develop a degree of natural rhythm with my clients. I pay particular attention to my clients' language, their speaking rhythms, their metaphors, and their body language as I mirror my own engagement with them. This allows me to experience my clients empathically and to engage them in a way that is consistent with their unique style. Too often we presume that all therapists know how to make their clients feel comfortable and safe. Yet each couple is different and will need a slightly different approach. With some couples I joke and with others I am deadly serious. Some people blossom when given empathy and nurturance; others simply shrug off empathic responses. Sometimes I swear like a sailor and sometimes I am as prim as a parson. We need to take our cues from our clients. They will teach us how to work with them.

> FRANK   We were a little nervous about this being on TV and all.
> D.T.   Can't say as I blame you. I always get a little nervous in these situations.
> FRANK   Sue said that she was sure that she was gonna say something dumb. Didn't ya, honey?
> D.T.   Well, don't worry about that. I know that I will say something dumb. Something always comes out wrong. But feel free not to talk about things that make you too uncomfortable. I think it's important for you not to feel like you have to talk about things that are really private between you two.

Entering Through the Family-of-origin Door

While getting to know the spouses, I will often ask general questions about their families of origin. One of my favorite questions, because it elicits so much information, is: How do you think your marriage is better or worse than your parents' marriage? I also ask about possible substance abuse in the family of origin as a matter of course.

> D.T.   Did any of your parents or siblings have problems with drugs or alcohol?
> SUE   Neither of my parents had much to do with alcohol. It was never a big deal in our house.
> FRANK   Well, I would have to say that my Mom was definitely an alcoholic.
> D.T.   Did she ever get treated for the problem?
> FRANK   Oh sure, we finally all got together and told her she'd have to go into the hospital or AA because we just couldn't stand it anymore. She'd get drunk and call up any of us kids and want to talk your ear off in the middle of the night. She always had a problem after she married my stepfather, but it really got bad after we all left home. That's when the phone calls started. We all knew she was lonely and we felt sorry for her but finally we had to put our foot down if you know what I mean.

> D.T. It sounds like you and your family realized that she couldn't do it on her own and that she needed a push from the people who cared about her.
>
> FRANK She sure wasn't going to stop by herself.
>
> D.T. What do you think, Sue? Do people in trouble with alcohol ever stop on their own or do they end up needing a loving push from the people the're close to?
>
> SUE I don't know much about it. I know they're supposed to want to stop first. But I don't know much about that.
>
> D.T. That's true. The trick is always figuring out what it's going to take to get somebody to want to stop, especially if the drinking problem hasn't really gotten too far out of control. Has your Mom been able to stay sober, Frank?
>
> FRANK Well, pretty much. She's had a few slips from time to time but she gets right back on track.
>
> D.T. Does she use AA as a support?
>
> FRANK No, she pretty much does it on her own and she gets some support from my aunt, her sister.
>
> D.T. Well, a lot of people have difficulty in using AA. I think most of us have too much pride to easily admit that we can't handle drinking and need to go to meetings in order to stop. I think walking through the doors of AA is one of the hardest things that you ever have to do.

Naturally, it is not always this easy to get the topic on the table. I remember one case in which bringing up the issue of parental drinking led to a fight between the spouses over whether or not his Dad was an alcoholic. Nevertheless, discussing the subject of substance abuse in the family of origin is easier than going directly to the question of substance abuse in the couple. It would have been a very different and probably much more difficult interview if I had waded in with direct questions about whether Frank and Sue had any problems with drugs and alcohol. Discussing how Frank's mother gave up drinking allows me to address many issues about the disease, change, and recovery without seeming to confront Frank or align with Sue. Interviewing them about his mother also allows me to elicit their ideas about alcoholism and recovery. It is very useful to discover that Frank generally does not believe that people go sober on their own.

The other reason for first raising the issue of substance abuse in the family of origin is that it allows me to engage the spouse who had an alcoholic parent around some of the difficulties of growing up in an alcoholic family. One of the main lines of defense for many people in early trouble with substance abuse is their conviction that their drinking is nowhere near as out of control as their alcoholic parent's. Rather than seeing the potential risks of their substance abuse, they tend to defend it, almost as if to say, "I had to put up with it as a kid and now it is my turn to be the drinker." In this case my task is to help Frank see the dangers of his own chemical use without accusing him of being the same as his alcoholic parent. Opening up these issues allows me to make an implicit appeal to the part of Frank that knows what it is like to be on the receiving end of substance abuse and does not want to repeat the pattern.

> D.T.   It must have been very tough for you to have to be the one who took care of your mother in that way.
>
> FRANK   She sure wasn't a pretty sight when she was into her whiskey.

Tracking

In the interview with Frank and Sue, the reward for the prolonged discussion about Frank's mother's drinking and my empathy with the difficulty of his position was that he volunteered that drinking was an issue between himself and Sue. Usually I have to make the transition myself, asking clients directly about their use of substances. I generally look for a way to ask about patterns of substance use as part of the discussion around the presenting problem. For example, in the case of Joan and Hank, who came in with a "communication" problem, I asked directly whether they communicated better or worse when either of them was using chemicals. Joan acknowledged that it was easier to listen to Hank when she was using pot. If spouses complain about fighting, I might ask them if their fighting is worse when either of them has been drinking.

Using the circular questioning developed by Palazzoli et al. allows me to track the role of substance abuse in the system without attacking anyone. This involves asking a series of questions that elicit descriptions of how things work in the family. By asking each member of the system to compare and contrast the behavior and feelings of other members, the therapist can begin to weave together a pattern of interaction in the family without assigning cause or blame. This introduces the notion of circularity and mutuality into what is often a highly reactive and blaming system. The pattern of substance abuse is addressed in a neutral and nonthreatening manner by such questions as: When Frank is drinking, who in the family becomes more involved with him and which family members become less involved with him? Which member of the family is most effective in showing their concern about your drinking without attacking you? In what ways is your drinking similiar to your Mom's and in what ways is it different?

My goals in carefully tracking the pattern of substance abuse with circular questioning are to learn how the substance abuse pattern works, to make it safe to talk about it, and to expose the connection between the substance abuse and other problems in the family without passing judgment. Implicit in the process are new ways to think about the problem.

D.T.   In what ways does your drinking cause fights between you and Sue?

FRANK   Well, when it comes to starting fights, I would have to say that Sue is always on my case about how many beers I've had and I think she counts every single one that comes out of the refrigerator. So we get into fights about that.

D.T.   I'm also wondering about what you two would tend to be fighting about if you didn't have this drinking issue to debate?

FRANK   I'd have to say that maybe we would have more fights about the sex business because it's not going anywhere and we don't talk about it much.

Therapeutic Alignment

It is almost always the case that, when one spouse has a substance abuse problem, both will assume that the nonabusing spouse and the therapist ally themselves against the abuser. This presumption of unbalanced alignment is usually there long before the couple has even met the therapist. It invariably leads the abuser to be defensive about his use of chemicals and/or critical of his spouse and her role in the problem. In order to get the issue out in the open in a nonthreatening way, I often begin by being somewhat critical or distant toward the spouse. I might suggest that she is using the issue as a weapon or is too judgmental in her approach to him. Thus, I overtly align myself with him by challenging her. This counterbalances their perception that I will automatically be her ally and enables me to elict his position on the substance abuse.

> FRANK Why don't you ask her about this stuff? She's the one who keeps track of my drinking. She knows exactly how much I drink.
>
> D.T. Well, Frank, I want Sue to stay out of this for the moment. It looks to me like she already butts in too much around this issue and I really want to know what you think about it.

On the surface I seem to be critical of Sue; yet in actuality I am aligned with her since I am pursuing the drinking issue, which is her complaint and not a stated concern of his. By challenging her I make it easier for him to feel less threatened by me. The therapist has to be very careful not to overdo this manuever of joining the drinker and challenging the spouse. In the course of an interview I move back and forth in my alliances with the spouses so that at the end they should have experienced me as evenhanded and impartial.

Going too far in challenging the spouse will lose the case, since it is the spouse—not the drinker—who is likely to make sure that therapy continues. It is essential that they both leave the interview feeling supported and understood in their respective positions.

Reframing

Generally couples seeking treatment are engaged in a considerable amount of fault-finding and blaming. In substance-abusing systems, the more drinkers are blamed for all the problems, the more likely they are to feel threatened and mistreated, which leads to increased denial and defensiveness. Their spouses' hostility becomes another excuse to drink. In order to interrupt the endless cycle of recriminations I use reframing techniques. The heart of reframing involves the therapist's expressing the view that the actions and motivations of each spouse can be understood from a positive and often protective perspective. Pointing out to a husband who is mad at his wife for her nagging how scared she is and how desperately she wants to be helpful begins to reframe her nagging as concern. She can no longer be seen simply as a controlling bitch; he has to consider that she might possibly be a loving woman who is afraid for him and does not know how to help.

In many cases, the judicious use of the disease model allows for a positive reframe of the drinker's behavior. For most drinkers, being seen by their spouses as victims of a disease for which they are not responsible is a great improvement. Another basic reframe involves seeing the potentially protective consequences of someone's drinking behavior from a systemic perspective.

> D.T.   One of the things that concerns me about your position, Sue, is what might happen to you if Frank does go sober. At this point his drinking kind of gives you a fair reason to avoid the sexual issues. I would be worried that you might feel enormous pressure to be responsive once he does stop drinking.
>
> SUE   Well, it would be very hard for me if he actually gives up drinking. I mean, wouldn't he have a right to think that things should get better in that area too?

My biggest concern in working with Frank and Sue (and with any other couple in which I feel there are substance abuse issues) is to develop a working relationship with them before I begin to push for change in the substance abuse pattern. I want the spouses to experience the therapy room as a safe place where they can address issues around substance use and abuse without getting into an out-of-control round of mutual recrimination and without the therapist's taking sides. I may feel very strongly, as I did in Frank's case, that a client is an alcoholic who needs to give up drinking entirely, but it is essential for me to start where the couple is, rather than aggressively push my own position. Knowing the "right" answer is not enough. I often tell my students that the hard part of therapy is not having the lightbulb go on in my head; rather, it is the art of creating the context that allows the lightbulb to go on in the client's head.

Sails need to be reefed, hatches need to covered, and everything below has to be restowed. I always make a checklist. I want the boat to be set up just right. There's no way to tell how bad the storm will be or how long it will last. There's no way to make the boat truly safe.

I work hard at setting up the therapy and preparing a couple. Sitting with Frank and Sue, I had a strong sense they would have to weather a major crisis before there would be any significant change. They are good people who love each other. I wanted to protect them. I knew I couldn't.

3

Riding It Out: Couples Therapy, Part Two

Therapy begins with developing relationships, describing problems in a way that makes them workable, and arriving at mutual goals. Most of my cases that go badly seem to result from my starting on the wrong foot right from the first interview. It may be that I was missing an important person in the session or precipitated a crisis prematurely, or that we agreed upon some unattainable goals. I am much more concerned about setting up the therapy carefully than I am about blundering into the substance abuse thicket unprepared. Once it has become possible for the couple to address the pattern of interactions that substance use in a relatively safe and non-threatening manner, then I am in a position to begin working more directly on these issues.

The first stage of treatment begins when the substance abuse is still active and is acknowledged as part of the couple's problem. In this chapter I discuss the underlying hypotheses, goals, strategies and potential outcome of the therapy during this phase of the work.

STAGE 1: DISENGAGEMENT

Hypotheses

My first hypothesis is that the chemical abuse is inextricably intertwined with the couple's pattern of behavior. Invariably, whatever pattern of behavior the couple's system has evolved around the alcohol use has become part of the problem rather than part of the solution. Regardless of whether spouses collude, fight, or ignore the substance abuse, their behavior inadvertently props up the pattern of abuse.

Secondly, it is often the spouse of the substance abuser who takes the initiative to change. People in the throes of substance abuse are clearly having difficulty in taking responsibility for their own behavior. Spouses, who are already prone to feel guilty and responsible, will be more easily motivated by therapy to change their part of the pattern.

A major exception to this rule occurs when the substance abuser is a woman. The husbands of these women often leave rather than attempt to work on the relationship. Those husbands who stay in the marriage are usually in more extreme denial than their spouses and may even be more resistant to treatment. It is not surprising that many caretaker husbands have a substance abuse problem of their own that remains hidden behind their wives' more obvious problems.

The last hypothesis is that interventions that cause one spouse to change will inevitably necessitate some kind of shift in the couple system as a whole and therefore in the other partner. Interventions that successfully shift the co-dependent's behavior may not lead to the drinker's sobriety or even to a reduction in substance abuse. Often the abuser will drink *more* as a result of this shift. Nevertheless, the spouse's behavioral change will expose the drinking problem as an individual issue rather than simply a part of the couple dynamics — and that is essential.

Goals

The primary goals of the disengagement stage are to shift the responsibility for the drinking behavior back to the drinker and to help the spouse discontinue her standard responses to the substance abuse, responses which contribute to maintaining the substance abuse pattern. By helping the spouse shift her role, the therapist destabilizes the enabling pattern and thus puts the responsibility back on the drinker.

Strategies

After effectively joining the couple, I employ several basic strategies in my work with the spouses to shift her response pattern and make him responsible for his use of chemicals. In presenting these strategies, I discuss the series of possible interventions with the spouse first and then review the interventions with the substance abuser. It is important to note, however, that in the actual sessions I shift back and forth between the spouses. Further, I do not attempt to use all these strategies in the first interview.

With the co-dependent spouse, I work on five options: reversals, Al-Anon, Intervention, separation and no change. Throughout this section I will primarily refer to the drinker as the husband and to the spouse as the wife. Most of these strategies are the same if the gender of the user is reversed. At the end of the chapter, I discuss some of the important differences between treating the female substance abuser and treating the male.

Reversals. Regardless of how the spouse responds to the substance abuse, I encourage her to change her normal reaction pattern. If she is constantly angry and critical, I encourage her to become more detached and less blaming. If she is passive and enabling, then I encourage her to be more assertive and confrontational. For example, I might say to the long suffering wife who always sits and waits with a warm dinner ready for her husband who has stayed out late drinking: " I think you need to eat with the kids and leave his food in the refrigerator. He can cook it himself." I might suggest to the husband who routinely engages in fights with his wife while she is actively drinking that he not make himself so vulnerable to her when she cannot aedquately respond. I tell him to write down his feelings and give them to her in the form of a letter when she is sober and able to consider his feelings more carefully. I ask wives not to call the boss with excuses or to cover up for him with the children. I encourage them not to cancel social engagements because of their fear that their husbands might drink too much and then insist on driving home. I urge them to go ahead anyway with a plan about how to get home on their own.

For many spouses, these ideas about changing their response patterns are quite threatening. They are already in a state of constant fear about rocking the boat and possibly breaking up their families. They also are very aware of their partner's potential wrath if they do assert themselves in a different manner. Consequently, I choose very slight shifts that can be accomplished rather than dramatic reversals that might result in failure.

Before I continue discussing these interventions made with the spouse, a word needs to be said about the impact of these suggestions on the drinker, who is sitting in the room listening to them. These suggestions generally tend to elicit defensive, angry, and resistant behavior on the part of the user. Since this is a natural response, I prepare him for the suggestions that will be given to the spouse. I frequently ask the drinker first, "Is your wife's usual way of dealing with you all that you want it to be?" I try to get agreement that the wife's typical response not only is unhelpful but potentially makes the situation worse. Obviously, I am attempting to block the drinker's resistance to my coaching the spouse by focusing on the changes that the spouse need to make, as if the problems were primarily hers.

The other way I elicit the husband's cooperation is by asking him if he cares about his wife's anxiety and distress and if he would like to be helpful to her. This defines my work as help to her rather than an attempt to change him. I want him to take the position of aiding her in getting help with *her* part of the problem. Many drinkers will go along with this idea, because at least for the moment it takes the heat off them. For once their wives are being challenged about their own behavior. Anticipating and blocking the drinker's reactivity are essential to effective intervention with the spouse.

> D.T. Listen, Frank, I need to talk to Sue now about her part of the problem and I might make suggestions to her that you don't like or it may seem that I completely agree with her point of view about your drinking. Clearly, she has a lot of fear and anxiety about this whole thing. I hope you'll just bear with me while I try to help her with it.
>
> FRANK Better her than me.

Even if the husband is cooperative, as Frank was, it is useful to address the issue of a possible backlash after the interview. At the end of the session I frequently ask whether either of them is worried about the "car ride home." If there are residual resentments, I want to get them out in the open before the couple leaves. That allows me to smooth any ruffled feathers. In this early stage of treatment, I do not want to precipitate a crisis in the system. The working relationship with the couple is not yet strong enough for that.

Al-Anon. Regardless of whether both agree that there is a drinking problem, I will almost always encourage the spouse to try Al-Anon as part of what she can do to change her participation in the system. Most spouses of abusers feel trapped, isolated, and self-blaming. Al-Anon can be a very effective way for them to better understand themselves. It is important for them to feel the sense of community and support that comes from sharing a problem with others who are in the same boat. Many spouses initially are reluctant to go to Al-Anon, particularly if their husbands are unwilling to do anything about the problem themselves. Often they protest that it is unreasonable for them to have go to meetings when they are not the ones with the problem in the first place.

I push pretty hard on this issue, telling them that, if they want to convince their husbands of their genuine concern and wish to be helpful, then the most powerful statement they can make is their willingness to go to meetings regardless of whether the drinker is ready to go. I also prepare them for the philosophy of detachment they will hear in Al-Anon meetings. I encourage them to go for their husband's sake even though they will hear that eventually they should become more detached from their husbands. It is insulting to tell spouses that they should go to Al-Anon because they need it or because they have a disease too. These women are desperately trying to do the best they can to hold their families together and to save their marriages. Suggesting that they go to Al-Anon as an immediate way to help their husbands is a more motivating and syntonic message for them. In cases when the co-dependent is the husband, I also address his comfort level with joining a group that may be predominantly female. Often I try to a refer a man to a group in which I know there are several men.

D.T.   Let me ask you, Sue, have you been going to Al-Anon?
SUE   It's been suggested to me, but honestly, I haven't really been able to find the time.

D.T. I really think it's important for you to try some meetings, because it's one of the best ways that you can let Frank know how concerned you are about this issue and that you are willing to go the extra mile in order to help this issue get dealt with.

SUE   I know I should.

D.T. Well, tell me a little bit about what blocks you from going to the meetings, because I really need to understand that.

Intervention. The third major tactic in working with a co-dependent involves suggesting the potential value of doing an intervention in order to help the drinker see the destructive nature of his abuse. The intervention technique was developed by Vernon Johnson of the Johnson Institute and will be presented in great detail in the next chapter. It is designed to force an alcoholic to see clearly both the serious nature of his problem and his need for professional help. Based on the assumption that the alcoholic has difficulty seeing the consequences of his own behavior resulting from his use of alcohol, the technique brings together representatives from all walks of the drinker's life. These individuals—family members, friends, employers, etc.— spell out the damaging consequences of his abuse from a variety of perspectives. This obviously works best if the abuser's behavior has become dysfunctional in many aspects of his life, so that there is considerable collaboration among the individuals involved. We bring together the wife, the children, the in-laws, other family menbers, his best friends, and potentially his employer, family doctor, and minister. Together the group faces the alcoholic and confronts him with his behavior in a gentle and caring way and recites the facts about the disease of alcoholism.

Bringing up the idea of an intervention with a wife in front of her husband is a dramatic move in itself. Most spouses are initially quite taken aback by the large-scale nature of the technique. Frequently, this increases their willingness to reconsider previously resisted ideas, such as going to Al-Anon or doing some reversals, because they know they are not ready to consider something as overwhelming as an intervention. Ironically, the drinker is also likely to become less hostile to his wife's going to Al-Anon or her no longer keeping his dinner warm once he hears about this more dramatic alternative. I suggest this idea only if there is a strong chance that the substance abuser will not deal with his drinking on his own. At this point I simply want to foreshadow one of the alternatives that may be appropriate if all else fails. It is extremely important to introduce the concept of the intervention as an option to be used *if* it turns out that the drinker has the disease of alcoholism and is unable to help himself.

> D.T.   You know, Sue, it seems clear that Frank's Mom could not deal with her drinking until her family was convinced that she was an alcoholic and got together and confronted her with their love and concern. I know that Frank has said today that he's going to either control his drinking or give it up, but if it turns out that he is an alcoholic he may not be able to give it up on his own. Do you suppose that you might need to gather the people who really care about him together in order to give him a loving push?
>
> FRANK   (interrupting) Now, now, I don't think that something like that is going to be necessary. I mean, don't you think that's going a little too far?
>
> D.T.   I don't know, Frank. Maybe it is. You seem to me to be the kind of guy who would prefer to face this problem on your own without involving a lot of other people. Maybe you're right.

In the interview with Frank and Sue I mentioned the idea of an intervention rather casually and quickly backed off when I hit his resistance. Usually it doesn't come at all in the first interview. When I do bring it up, it generally makes the more modest alternatives much more acceptable.

Separation. Reversals and Al-Anon are appropriate options for all spouses, regardless of the severity of the substance abuse. Interventions and the separation option are called for when there is a very good chance that the drinker is completely unable to control his use of alcohol on his own. I encourage the spouse to consider separation as potentially her last option in helping her husband, protecting her children, and saving herself. At the same time I strongly assert that, rather than seeing separation as giving up on the alcoholic, she should understand it as in some cases the only way to save the alcoholic's life. The potential necessity of a separation comes up in the context of presenting to the spouse the disease model of alcoholism, with the implication that without a dramatic approach the alcoholic is going to fall victim to a progressive and terminal disease.

The idea of a separation is presented as the spouse's ultimate sacrifice rather than a move toward abandonment and divorce. This particular move obviously shakes the system to the core and, as in the case of the intervention, tends to make the spouse more willing to undertake less threatening behaviors. The alcoholic hearing the notion of separation discussed is likely to express considerable hostility. Having introduced this idea, I usually retreat to the possibility that the couple will not need to separate and that there may be other, less traumatic solutions to their problems.

The no-change option. My last technique to help the spouse disengage from her enabling role is to raise the possibility that she may not be able to change any of her habitual responses to her husband. Suggesting that maybe she is not ready to risk changing at all has to be done very respectfully, so that she does not experience me as being critical. I have to keep in mind the often desperate nature of the spouse's dilemma, and to empathize with her feelings of helplessness. Accepting her fear that, if she were to do anything different at all, she would be risking her marriage, her children, and her own future is an important intervention. The first step toward successful change is to take responsibility for one's current behavior. If I help a spouse decide that she is not ready to change because of the compelling nature of the risks involved, then at least I have helped her make a choice. She is no longer defining herself as a victim. Deciding to do nothing is doing something.

Frequently this option propels the client either to attempt to talk the therapist into giving her more suggestions for things she can do or to initiate spontaneously some change that the therapist has not suggested. Even if the couple were to decide to leave therapy at this point, this particular maneuver would increase the wife's unwillingness to accept the status quo indefinitely and create pressure for future change.

This technique is useful when all other suggestions are greeted with "yes, but" responses. Many clients come to us in a state of impasse; they are like rabbits frozen in the glare of oncoming headlights. It is important for us not to overreact to the "yes, but" position, instead appreciating the desperate anxiety that leads them to become frozen in their tracks.

Clearly, these strategies must be used with sensitivity to the spouse's position. I assume that all of my clients are ambivalent about the risks of change. They are both genuinely desirous of new solutions and afraid of trying something different. It is our job to make change safe and fear acceptable. When trying to think of recommendations that will not seem too risky to clients, I remember the Confucian line, "A journey of ten thousand miles begins with a single step."

My work with the spouse is related to my work with the substance abuser. Whether I work first with husband or wife depends on the results of the initial stages of joining the couple and tracking the role of substance abuse in the system. My rule of thumb is to work first with the most motivated person in the room. In most cases, this will be the spouse of the substance abuser.

While I encourage the spouse to detach from her role, I help the abuser take more responsibility for his use of chemicals. It is important for me to approach the abuser's behavior from a nonjudgmental position. If I convey a sense of urgency about the abuser's behavior my perceived alignment with the spouse will be confirmed in his mind. This will significantly decrease the abuser's willingness to look at his own behavior with an open and inquiring attitude.

My job is to help the drinker to evaluate the consequences of drinking both to himself and to others and then to make a careful decision about whether he should stop drinking, moderate his drinking, or continue to drink at the present level and risk the consequences. I save confrontation for later, when I have built a solid relationship with the abuser. I do not assume that my clients are incapable of assessing their own behavior and potential problem with substances. I start with the premise that they are competent and responsible people who care about themselves and others. I am not asking them to change and I'm not blaming them for all the problems in their relationships. All I'm asking them to do is consider, using their own criteria, whether they have any problems with chemicals. This quite benign approach rather than an educational or confrontational method, usually enables clients to cooperate in the early stages of therapy.

There are four specific options that I consider if the client thinks
that his use of chemicals is not a real problem: observational drinking, chemical dependency consultation, controlled drinking contracts, and therapeutic termination.

Observational drinking. This first option is used when the
drinker is actively denying that there is any drinking problem at all.
In the case of Frank and Sue, he had already acknowledged that
drinking was an issue and that perhaps he should do something
about it. In many cases, however, the drinker categorically denies
any problem. The abuse may not even be considered a problem by
the spouse. In these situations, I simply track carefully the user's
perception about the effect on him and on his spouse of his use of
alcohol or drugs. With the user I develop a series of hypotheses
about what substance use does for him. What is he looking for in
the martini at the end of the day? What kind of shift of mood is he
trying to achieve? How does he feel if he is unexpectedly unable to
drink at a time when he normally would? What about his use of
chemicals worries him? How would he know if he did have a
problem with chemicals?

In listening to his answers to these questions, I must remain
uncritical. It undercuts my effort to encourage him to take responsibility for his behavior if I start off by confronting all of his
positions. I assume that the abuser is not fully conscious of what
he expects to achieve from his use of chemicals, the rigidity of his
pattern of use, and his underlying dependency. Actively observing
one's use of alcohol is a major first step in taking more responsibility.

Asking clients these kinds of observational questions leads quite
natually to my assigning homework tasks which encourage them
to continue the observational process. They are asked to keep a
drinking log in which they enter the amount of each drink, the
time of day, and what they hoped to experience as a result of
having the drink. Many substance abusers resist keeping a log or
agree to do it and then forget all about it, but those clients who
actually use the log find it to be an extremely powerful learning
tool. They begin to recognize the important role that drinking
plays in their lives and the degree to which they are dependent on
their particular pattern of substance use.

With those clients who refuse to do the log or "forget" to do it, I raise questions about what would be uncomfortable for them about watching their drinking behavior closely. Whether clients do the assignment or not, the homework enables me to keep the drinking out in the open without taking a confrontational position. It helps me establish the idea that ultimately the abuser is responsible for his own use and for dealing with the consequences of that use to himself and the others around him.

Chemical dependency consultation. If my client expresses some concern about his pattern of abuse, but I want to avoid pushing him directly, lest I appear to be aligning with his wife against him, then I encourage him to consult an expert on chemical dependency. This enables him to get an outside opinion and perhaps to learn that he has a serious problem that needs treatment, without being browbeaten into it. Many people struggling with their inability to control their chemical use need to feel that they have dealt with the problem on their own. Seeing the chemical dependency expert is often a face saving way for the individual to acknowledge the problem. Naturally, if I think a client is in serious trouble, I will refer him to a colleague who is not likely to be misled by the client's minimizing of the issue.

Controlled drinking contracts. When the client acknowledges that there are problems but feels that he is basically in control of his drinking and that his spouse is blowing the issue way out of proportion, I usually pursue the idea of drawing up a controlled drinking contract with the drinker. The purpose of a controlled drinking contract is to establish the drinker's position of being responsible for setting his own standards for his alcohol use. I encourage the drinker to use the concept of the contract to demonstrate that he is in control of his chemical use.

Controlled drinking contracts are filled with natural pitfalls; I have learned from painful experience how easy it is to be manipulated when doing them. One client, for example, successfully kept to his two-glasses-of-wine-per-day contract—it wasn't until after the contract had been in place for two months that the wife told me that he was drinking each "glass" of wine in a brandy snifter. No wonder he was having no problem with the contract. He was successfully imbibing a bottle and a half of wine each night. Another client's four beers a day turned out to be four quart bottles of beer. He wasn't complaining about his limit either.

It has also become evident that many clients do not apply the designated daily drinking limit to "special" days when there might be a party, a problem at the office, a fight with the wife, or a World Series game on TV. Finally, clients are sometimes less than honest about complying with the contract. When caught exceeding their limit, they invariably managed to embroil me in a debate about whether one small little slip is really anything to get all that excited about.

From these experiences, I have developed a way of setting up a controlled drinking contract that usually works. The first step is to get the client to agree to the maximum amount of alcohol per day that he will imbibe regardless of external events or provocations. He agrees that, if he exceeds this amount, then that means he has a serious drinking problem and will either stop drinking or seek help to significantly reduce his drinking. Amounts are determined by numbers of drinks. One twelve ounce can of beer, one shot of hard liquor, and one small glass of wine are all defined as equivalent to "one drink." I encourage the spouse to go along with the contract, but I warn her that he may come up with a level of daily drinking that is simply unacceptable to her. If this is the case, we will have to address the issue in therapy. First we see if he can keep the contract; then we deal with the question of whether the wife can live with it and whether it is a safe amount of alcohol.

In the session with Frank and Sue, I negotiated a controlled drinking contract. I will use the transcript to show the steps of this process with a couple.

> D.T.   I mean, what's your idea of a maximum amount of alcohol per day that you could stick to come hell or high water?
>
> FRANK   A maximum, huh? I've tried that, but I've always set something that was way too low.
>
> D.T.   Well, that's what people usually do. But what you need to do is really come up with an amount that you believe is right for you. I remember one guy who came up with a maximum of two double scotches plus one case of beer per day.
>
> FRANK   (laughing) I think I might know that guy.
>
> D.T.   Anyway, how much do you think is the right amount for you per day?

FRANK   Well, I don't drink any more than five or six a night. I'd have to say a six pack would be about right.

D.T.   What about on weekends or holidays?

FRANK   You mean during the day, too?

D.T.   Sure.

FRANK   Well, if it's a nice day and maybe I'm working outside and all, then maybe I might have another six-pack.

D.T.   So a genuine maximum limit that would cover weekends and holidays would be a total of two six-packs, 12 beers. Is that right?

FRANK   Yep.

D.T.   And if you drank more than that, you would agree that that means you have a real problem with alcohol and that you would need to stop drinking and go to AA. Is that right?

FRANK   I would be ready to do that, yep.

D.T.   Here's a tough one for you. Suppose you drank 13 beers. Would that mean that you needed to stop drinking?

FRANK   Now you're getting tough on me.

D.T.   You've got that right. I just want to make sure that we make a deal that you believe in, that is really a fair test for you. Should we make it a higher limit, say 15 beers?

FRANK   No, I think 12 is about right.

D.T.   What do you think, Sue? Do you think that if we agree to 12 Frank will stick to it? Or do you think that a couple of months from now, if an old buddy from Vietnam shows up and they really get plastered, then he'll turn around and say that one screwup doesn't really count?

SUE   Frank's pretty good about keeping to his word. Now, I don't know about two months from now.

D.T.   Well, what we're trying to do here is come up with a deal that Frank will stick to no matter how long. There should be no excuses for breaking the deal. In other words, no matter what happens, Frank would stay within that 12-beers-a-day limit. Is that clear to you, Frank?

FRANK   I think I can do that. I won't say that I've never had more than two six-packs, but this seems more than fair to me. I'm not so sure that Sue is going to like it.

D.T.   I'm glad you brought that up, because in truth Sue doesn't have to like it. It is important for you to really discover whether or not you can set a limit and stick to it, because that's possibly the best way for you to find out that you're not in charge of your beer or maybe the beer is in charge of you. I

mean two six-packs a day is a lot of alcohol; frankly, I personally think it is way too much for you to be drinking. But what
we're doing is trying to help you find out if you can limit
yourself to that amount. If you can, you may still decide that
you should drink considerably less than that. If you can't I
think you're going to be smart enough to get yourself into AA
instead of going all the way down the tubes like your mother
did.

    What I want you to understand, Sue, is that if Frank does
keep to his limit, then you will have to decide whether or not
that amount of daily alcohol is something you can live with.
It's possible that he will succeed at this limit. Then the ball
will be in your court. Some people could go on for years
drinking two six-packs a day.

FRANK (interrupting) No one said that I had to drink two six
packs every single day.

D.T. That's true, Frank. All I'm saying to Sue is that if you are
able to stick to this contract and you feel that that amount of
booze is okay with you, then she'll have to decide whether
that's an amount she can handle.

Obviously, negotiating these contracts is a rather delicate balancing act. I want the limit to be high enough so that if the drinker
fails then he genuinely fails by his own criteria, not mine or his
wife's. At the same time, I do not want to be seen as inadvertently
endorsing a level of inappropriate alcohol abuse. Nor do I want the
wife to think that she has to accept the limit just because he suc-
ceeds in sticking to it. The power of this intervention is manifest in
its impact on the spouse. Usually spouses perceive the alcohol
abuse as something that happens from time to time because of
mitigating circumstances. Listening to her husband consciously
spell out a program that permits a very high level of alcohol use is
usually thoroughly unnerving. I need to be sensitive to how difficult it is to sit through this process. The wife will often be on the
edge of walking out of the room. A controlled drinking contract
such as the one made with Frank tends to break down the wife's
denial and willingness to continue enabling behavior; this is, in
fact, a key purpose of the contract.

    Sometimes drinkers actually keep the contract, following
through with AA or alcoholism counseling when they go over their

limit. Typically, however, the drinker is unable to stay within the limit and is unwilling to accept the consquences. This leads to a major confrontation with the spouse. It is frequently this failure on the husband's part that gives the wife the sufficient motivation to move in the direction of either an intervention or a therapeutic separation. My response to the husband's failure is to suggest that his alcohol use is simply a problem that cannot be solved by will-power and limit-setting. This is the ideal time to reinforce the disease concept as a way of benignly reframing why the drinker has no choice but to continue to break the contract. The inability to keep the contract becomes the evidence that the drinker is being controlled by the drink. I usually say to him at this point that he shouldn't be too hard on himself about it; after all, it's not a failure of character or commitment. It's just that he has hasn't understood the nature of the disease. My basic message is: "You can't strength-en a broken leg by running on it and you can't control drinking by willpower."

The most problematic outcome is when the drinker successfully stays within his chosen, dangerously high limit and thus feels that he has proven that his alcohol use is under control. This does not happen often, since most people in trouble with chemicals are not able to stay within any limit for very long. When they do keep the contract, I work with the spouse on helping her define what she can tolerate. At this point I may confront the drinker with my own perception that he has set a level of daily alcohol or drug use that is dangerous for him and clearly hurtful to his marital relationship. I recall having to tell one client that I truly regretted ever making the contract with him, since it seemed obvious that I had made it easier for him to continue drinking in a self-destructive manner.

Therapeutic termination. In cases where the drinker continues to insist on a level of drinking that I feel is inappropriate, then I carefully and gently decline further treatment. If I have successfully built a good relationship with the drinker and treated him with respect throughout the process, then ending the therapy usually has a profound impact. At this critical juncture, I explain to the client that often therapy can become part of the problem instead of being part of the solution, and that it is personally important for me not to be in the position of enabling alcoholism by continuing treatment. I tell the story of the alcoholic who came to see me after 10 years of therapy in which he and the therapist attempted to get to the root causes of his drinking. In this way I explain how sometimes therapy allows people to continue to drink while believing that they are really trying to do something about the problem.

Even if the therapeutic termination of a case does not generate a shift in the drinker's behavior, it usually mobilizes the spouse to become less willing to continue her enabling behavior. Suddenly she faces the possibility of being alone again with the problem. At this point I might again suggest doing an intervention or encourage her to get some individual therapy in order to get strong enough to confront her husband. I make it clear to the couple that I remain committed to them and am willing to resume treatment after the client gives up drinking.

AA, abstinence, and inpatient treatment. When clients recognize the problem and are seeking help, I recommend that they try a series of AA meetings to find out if they can successfully abstain from substance abuse. A minimum of six meetings is a prerequisite for any kind of successful joining between the individual and an AA groups. Since AA meetings are frequently intimidating and uncomfortable, encouraging clients to take their time and shop around for the right AA group is extremely useful. I also tell my clients not to worry about whether they have to give up drinking forever. In AA, you don't have to be committed to abstinence in order to go to meetings and you only work on "one day at a time." In addition, clients needn't worry about buying all of the program in order to benefit from AA. I also find it helpful to match a client up with an AA member so that they can meet before my client's first meeting and then go together.

I am quite cautious about suggesting that clients maintain a period of abstinence as a strategy. Many clients have already used periodic abstinence as a means of demonstrating that they aren't alcoholics. In these cases the period of abstinence is followed by continued abuse in the same old pattern. When recommending abstinence as an experiment I usually tell my clients a minimum of 60 days is necessary.

When clients are interested in going sober but undecided about whether to use AA or an inpatient treatment center, I usually recommend inpatient treatment as a good way to start. For many people an inpatient setting—a complete break in routines and normal context—often makes the first month of sobriety easier to attain. I particularly like programs that engage the families intensively in the treatment process, such as the pioneering family program at St. Mary's Hospital in Minneapolis. One should recognize, however, that many people effectively go sober using AA on an outpatient basis and that participation in inpatient treatment provides no guarantee of success.

Outcome

All these strategies designed to disengage the spouse and to make the substance abuser responsible for his own behavior and chemical use do not necessarily lead to recovery. Generally people go sober because of considerable external pressure. These interventions are all designed to intensify the external pressure while breaking down the covert collusion in the couple system that protects the abuser.

Storms at sea are always hard to weather. The boat lurches and shudders. The constant beating of wind, spray, and rain wears you down. Sea sickness, hunger, and fear twist your stomach. Through the night, the roaring noise envelops you. You get tired, cold, and scared. You keep waiting for the one big wave that will knock the boat over.

At this stage in the couples treatment, the crisis that usually takes place does not feel controllable. I try to assess the risks of physical abuse, suicide, and self-endangering behavior as the pressure for change builds on each member of the couple. At the same time I try not to squelch the process out of my own anxiety. Usually there's no way to turn back. It's just a matter of riding it out.

About half of the couples that I see come out of the crisis and go into some form of recovery program. Approximately a quarter resolve the issue, with the substance abuser learning how to use chemicals more moderately and the couple working on their other relationship issues. Unfortunately, the rest either divorce or withdraw from treatment without significant change.

*   *   *   *   *

I have not been able to find out what happened to Frank and Sue. It felt as if it had been a good interview. Some months later I learned that the couple had experienced an intensification around the drinking issue because, ironically, Frank's daughter was arrested for a D.U.I.

The other day, I tried to call the therapist who had treated Frank and Sue and discovered that she had moved and the phone company had no forwarding address. Being left with this kind of ambiguity is typical. Maybe Frank is sober and the whole family is in recovery. Maybe they're divorced. Maybe they're completely unchanged. I would feel better if I knew what happened, and yet it's not unusual for us not to know the ultimate impact of our work. It is our odd fate to be major actors in the drama of people's lives and yet frequently to miss the ending.

As the boat gently rocks in the bright sunshine the morning after the storm, there's a moment of wonder. Was it just a dream?

4

Endgame: Using the Intervention Technique

In the living room are her siblings, children and grandchildren, her colleagues, husband, and friends. They are all waiting for her. There is very little social chatter in the room. Many are reading to themselves from notes they have in their hands. The children are actively fidgeting, while the grownups cross and uncross their legs. People keep looking at the clock.

She is a matriarch, a community leader, and vice president of the local bank. She has locked herself in the bathroom. Her son is standing at the bathroom door pleading with her to come out. "You need help," he says plaintively. "I don't need any help. I can take care of this on my own," she responds defiantly. The son continues to plead and the mother refuses to budge. The people in the living room sit silently.

Finally, I go to the door and say, "Mrs. Harrison, you may not need to have this meeting but the people out here are all feeling embarrassed and anxious. They have all told me how gracious you are and how you always go out of your way to make people feel comfortable. They seem to care for you a lot and they have gone to great lengths to prepare for this meeting. I think it would really help them if you would let them talk with you."

After a moment of silence, the bathroom door swings open and Mrs. Harrison marches out. "Well," she says, "If it would make them all feel better, let's get on with it."

At first she sits with a kind of stony set to her face as people go around in a circle reading from their prepared statements.

The eldest daughter reads, "Mother, I love you and I miss the way you used to be. I always looked up to you and I never would have been able to go to graduate school and take care of my kids without your love and support.

"I'm here because I want to tell you how worried I am about your drinking. I am afraid that the way you drink is ruining your life. It is certainly getting in the way of our relationship. I would like you to know some of the things that have happened that I think were caused by your drinking.

"I remember your calling me in the middle of the night three years ago and telling me to call the police because there was a burglar in the house. The police and I rushed over to the house and when we got there you were obviously drunk and told the police that of course there weren't any burglars. You said you couldn't imagine why I would have made up such a story and dragged the police department out in the middle of the night on such a wild goose chase. I was so embarrassed. I just knew that you would never act like that if you weren't drunk.

"You have been complaining that you don't see enough of your grandchildren in the summertime. For the last few summers I have been making up excuses for why we don't stay very long with you on the Cape. The real reason is that you start drinking at 10 o'clock in the morning and by noon you are drunk and I don't trust you to be with my kids. When you are drinking you become nasty and mean and I don't want my kids to grow up thinking that you are like that.

"I guess I really began to know that you were an alcoholic five years ago when I was at your house at Thanksgiving time. I came down in the morning to give you a hand with the turkey. It was very early and I knew you would be the only one up. I came into the kitchen and there you were with your back to me pouring yourself a glass of wine. When you saw me you got mad and accused me of sneaking up on you.

"There's much more I could say, Mom, because these things have been going on for a long time. But all I really want to tell you is that I love you and I really hope that you will get help because I think that the way you are drinking is wrecking your life. I'm sorry if my saying all this is hurtful to you. I'm only saying these things because I love you and want you to get better."

The daughter stops reading and begins to cry. Her mother stares off into space with an angry, defiant set to her jaw. There is an awkward silence in the room as all stare at the floor and wait their turn.

After several more in the group read their statements it is Allison's turn. Allison is sitting bolt upright in her chair. She is staring down at the paper clutched in her hands. She begins to read in a forced and stilted fashion from the page. She is eight years old.

"I love you MayMay and I know that you are sick and need to get help. Mom said I didn't have to come to this meeting but I said that I wanted to because I want you to get better.

"Some of the things that I remember are when you slapped Jonathan just because he had spilled some milk on the rug. And sometimes in the summer when you take us to the beach, you drive the car all over the road and I get scared you are going to run into a telephone pole or another car. And after you have some drinks, you talk funny and you seem to forget who I am."

Allison stops reading and looks at her grandmother and says directly, "Please stop drinking, MayMay. Please."

Mrs. Harrison slumps in her chair and puts her hands over her eyes. She begins to cry. Her best friend, who is sitting next to her, takes her hand.

I was not at all sure that this group was going to be able to reach Mrs. Harrison; however, when she responded to her grandaughter, I knew that finally she was going to accept treatment. At that point almost everyone in the room was in tears. So was I.

Interventions are dramtic, emotional, and tough. When the alcoholic is denying the problem, the intervention approach is often the only alternative to giving up. It's the last move.

Alcoholism is characterized by the alcoholic's usually being unable to see the destructive consequences of his drinking behavior either to himself or to others. The intervention technique is a process where the people who care most deeply for an alcoholic and believe that he or she has a serious problem with drinking meet with a professional and are taught how to collectively express their concern and their desire that the alcoholic go into some kind of treatment. It holds up to the alcoholic in a loving and firm manner a mirror showing the impact of alcohol on his/her behavior and relationships. It also makes clear the unwillingness of family and friends to continue to participate in the abuse without taking some kind of action in response.

Until this technique was developed by Vernon Johnson in the early seventies and described in his book, *I'll Quit Tomorrow* it was generally assumed in the alcoholism field that alcoholics had to "hit bottom" before they would engage in treatment. "Hitting bottom" meant losing one's spouse, family, health, driver's license, or job, or all of the above. It was thought that such a sharp blow to the stability of the alcoholic's system was essential for the alcoholic to see the consequences of his drinking and to seek help. The intervention process creates such a destabilization by providing tough confrontation with the reality of the destructive course of drinking before the predictably tragic events have happened. The confrontation with family, friends, relatives, etc., is a little like Scrooge's encounter with the ghosts of Christmases past, present, and future. Like Scrooge, the alcoholic is given the opportunity to make changes and avert fate.

When interventions are well organized and prepared, there is a high success rate in terms of helping alcoholics accept treatment. Mrs. Harrison, who initially would not come out of the bathroom, flew the next day halfway across the country to a Midwest treatment center, where she spent a month. In the seven years following the intervention she has not had a drop to drink.

Mrs. Blair is a different story. Mrs. Blair will die a bitter, angry alcoholic. She, too was confronted by an intervention and went into inpatient treatment. It is evident that she will never forgive her family for imposing that treatment on her and for the profound sense of shame, betrayal, and humiliation that she experienced in the intervention process. The intervention and the resulting hospitalization have become another excuse to drink. She will carry her resentment to the grave.

Powerful therapeutic procedures often achieve dramatic results and dramatic failures. When I was first exposed to the intervention technique 10 years ago, I was quite uncomfortable with it. At that time therapists were diagnosing alcoholism by talking over the phone with the spouse of a drinker, meeting secretly with family members, and then taking the alcoholic by surprise in a meeting that sometimes seemed like an ambush. For example, one man coming downstairs in his bathrobe looking for the paper at 7 o'clock on a Sunday morning was greeted by his family and closest friends, who were waiting for him in the living room. In addition, as a family therapist I was disconcerted by the implications of this approach that the problems in the family are completely attributable to alcoholism and that the designated alcoholic's perspective may simply be denied by calling everything he has to say "denial." There also seemed to be a high potential for destructive polarization of families by the technique. Even if inpatient treatment were achieved, the long term process of family healing might be quite difficult.

Over the years, as I have learned how to do interventions, I have adapted the procedure to make it more consistent with my normal way of working with families. In the following pages I answer some of the basic questions about this approach and how I use it.

WHEN DO YOU USE THE INTERVENTION TECHNIQUE?

I use the intervention technique when the alcoholic family member refuses to take part in any kind of treatment, when the alcoholic denies the seriousness of the drinking problem and its impact on the family, when I have been working with the family and the alcoholic drops out of treatment, and when other therapists refer families to me specifically for this procedure. I will not do interventions when family members have not already tried to talk with the alcoholic about the drinking on their own or when significant family members are unwilling to participate. My biggest concern is whether the potential intervention group will be able to participate in the procedure in a positive and powerful manner. My criteria for a good working group vary from case to case, but some of the key ones are:

(1) a high level of motivation on the part of the group;
(2) representation in the group of many different aspects of the drinker's life, i.e., family, friends, co-workers, and relatives;
(3) unity among the group about the seriousness of the drinking problem and the need for treatment;
(4) the ability of the group to show genuine love and concern for the individual while taking a strong position against the alcoholism.

Interventions work best when families are desperate, when they feel like they have tried everything and nothing has worked, when they are willing to do *whatever it takes*. Ironically, this means that interventions work most effectively for alcoholics who have not progressed so far into their disease that they have lost the support of friends and family. People in the end stages of alcohol abuse have frequently lost some significant parts of their support system, so that there is not a very strong intervention network to call upon. They've been divorced, lost their job, or don't have any friends who are not abusive drinkers themselves. On the other hand, alcoholics who are in the early stage of their addiction will tend to be inappropriate for an intervention precisely because their drinking has not yet become disruptive in most aspects of their lives. A key, often successful defense for drinkers resisting treatment is to point to their performance in some significant area, such as work or home life, and to claim that the fact that they don't have problems in that area proves that they are not alcoholic. Interventions seem to work most effectively for abusers in the middle of their course of addiction, i.e., after the problem has become clear to many people in their network and before they lose the love and support of family, friends and colleagues.

What Are the Basic Steps of an Intervention?

(1) Assessment

When I am asked to do an intervention I start with an assessment process. First I invite the concerned family members to a meeting. I ask them to invite the drinking member to join them; if they are reluctant to invite him or her, I ask them to at least inform the abuser that such a meeting is taking place. Usually family members are extremely anxious about confronting the drinker and therefore uncomfortable about having him/her come to the first session. It is, however, important that the drinker know about the process and be allowed to participate if he/she chooses. Telling the drinker about the meetings announces from the start that the intervention is not a conspiracy being conducted behind the back of the alcoholic; rather, it is being handled in an open and direct fashion. Obviously, family members and friends worry that the drinker might be quite provoked and hostile about the whole idea; therefore it is important that they be coached carefully about how to broach the subject in the first place. The following is a letter that one client wrote her husband.

Dear Bob,

I want you to know that I love you very much and that I am very worried about you. We have had many fights about your drinking and I feel desperately unsuccessful in the way that I have been responding to you. I am sure that my complaining about your drinking all the time only makes the situation worse.

I have decided to get some professional help to learn what I and the children can do to be more supportive and loving in how we express our concern about your drinking. If you would like to come to the meeting that would be fine, but if not I just want to reassure you that we are going because we love you and want to help you. Clearly what we are doing now isn't helpful at all and we need some guidance as to what we can perhaps be doing differently.

Love,

Alice

In cases where there is a risk of physical retaliation or some other destructive response I respect the family members' wish not to invite the drinker to the early meetings. The principle of having the process open and aboveboard has to be balanced with a concern for people's safety. In one family, the wife and children had to move out of the house to a safe location before they felt protected enough to confront the alcoholic husband.

In this initial assessment I take a drinking history, find out who in the individual's network is actively concerned and willing to help, explore the impact of the drinking behavior on others, and evaluate prior attempts to deal with the drinking issue. It is not unusual to discover in an initial meeting that no one has ever really talked to the drinker directly; that significant family members, such as the drinker's children, completely deny that there is any problem; or that the amount of drinking at issue is genuinely very moderate. In one case, a young woman called and asked for an intervention to be done on her fiancé before she married him. I talked with her at some length over the phone before actually asking her how much the young man drank. In response she said, "Well, he drinks around three beers." I asked her if that was three every night, and she said, "Oh no, I couldn't stand him drinking every night. I mean he drinks three beers a week!" The question I did not ask, but perhaps I should have, was, "And how much does your father drink?"

Carefully evaluating the family's appropriateness for an intervention often leads to my encouraging family members to take some intermediate steps before deciding that an Intervention is the only alternative. Interventions are most effective when all agree that everything else has been tried and nothing has worked.

If the drinker has come to the first session, then I want to fully understand his position and to hear him articulate both his ideas of what is appropriate drinking for himself and his thoughts about how he would quit drinking if he thought he needed to stop. The initial strategy is to have the drinker take responsibility for his use of alcohol. This leads to the controlled drinking contract approach, as discussed in Chapter 3. Usually, when people request an intervention, the drinking and the family situation are well beyond the point of being handled with a controlled drinking approach. The family members may simply make a deal with the drinker that they will go along with his or her efforts to demonstrate ability to manage alcohol if he/she is willing to accept their need to do an intervention if he/she fails. In essence, what I'm trying to do is elicit the drinker's tolerance for the intervention.

D.T.   Mr. Blake, I think your wife and your kids really love you a lot. They seemed to be scared stiff that you were going to be mad at them for having this meeting. Are you going to resent their calling me and setting up this meeting?

MR. BLAKE   No, of course not.

D.T.   Good. The other thing is that they obviously have not been able to be helpful and it sounds like the way they deal with it has been hostile and blaming. There is a way that they can be taught how to express their love and concern for you that will not be an attack. But they're going to need for you to be willing to let them come to a few meetings to learn how to do that. Would that be all right?

MR. BLAKE   Frankly, I think this is a big waste of time and money and I'm not going to be coming back.

D.T.   It's fine if you would prefer not to come back. It will actually make it a little easier for them because they're clearly uncomfortable trying to talk about this stuff in front of you. We will need you to come back for the one meeting that I mentioned but in the meantime I will probably meet with them about three more times. If anything comes up during this period and you have any questions, please feel free to call me.

MR. BLAKE   I haven't said that I'm coming to any more meetings.

D.T.   I know, but I would guess that if it's really important to your wife and kids, you might come in one time just for them.

Who is winning? It is a draw; usually that's the best I can hope for. Alcoholics who do not want to be in treatment are frequently obstreperous and hostile. I try not to be intimidated, reactive, or too pushy. I show alcoholics the same respect and courtesy that I would show to anyone else. In addition, I want to demonstrate to the family that it is possible to work with an alcoholic without either fighting or submitting, i.e., that one can be gentle and respectful while being firm and assertive. This models for them the basic stance that is the essence of an intervention.

Another important benefit of including the alcoholic in this initial session is that it alleviates the family's anxiety about being disloyal and unfair. Whether the alcoholic is cooperative or obstructionist, family members can feel that they went the extra mile in trying to be fair and aboveboard with him/her. In the eventuality that the drinker begins to filibuster or intimidate, I ask him to help the family members deal with their anxiety and defensiveness by either coming to the meetings as a silent observer or skipping a couple of meetings while they learn how to express their concern without feeling totally exposed to the drinker's anger and criticism.

In most cases requiring interventions, these prescriptions about how to manage the alcoholic in the session are unnecessary, since the drinker refuses to attend the meetings anyway. Consequently, the main goals of the initial session are:

(1) establishing the appropriateness of an intervention;
(2) deciding who should participate;
(3) explaining how an intervention actually works;
(4) helping the family members anticipate and cope with the potentially hostile and destructive responses of the alcoholic.

Once it has been decided that an intervention is appropriate, selecting participants is critically important. Usually an intervention begins with a wife, a child, or a colleague calling and asking for help. There is often a strong inhibition around involving other people; the impulse to protect the alcoholic is a natural response on the part of the people closest to him. The boss will have a hard time telling the wife, the wife doesn't want to tell the boss, and the children don't want to talk with the drinker's brothers and sisters, their uncles and aunts. The key to developing a large enough cross-section of people to participate in the intervention is patience. It is not a lack of motivation that causes people to be anxious about involving others; rather, their anxiety is a legitimate expression of fear, embarrassment, and a sense of being disloyal. The therapist needs to respect this anxiety, building the group slowly if necessary. As more people are added to the group, the seriousness and pervasiveness of the drinker's problem become more obvious and the group becomes increasingly more committed and confident.

Many times a very significant family member is actively or covertly opposed to the intervention. In this case the group must find a way of confronting that person's resistance and encouraging his or her involvement. I have treated several cases where the grown children of an alcoholic have wanted to do an intervention and have been opposed by the alcoholic's spouse. Usually the spouse either denies the seriousness of the problem or has his/her own problem with drinking, which is only a little more under control than that of the designated alcoholic and likely to be exposed in the process. In those situations, I have done what amounts to two interventions—the first on the spouse and the second on the "alcoholic." If a significant family member will not participate, then an intervention is much less likely to be effective; however, it may be worthwhile doing it for the benefit of the group members, who need to express their concern and to feel that they have given it "their best shot."

During the assessment stage the therapist needs to be very cautious about encouraging an intervention. By appreciating ambivalence and accepting anxiety, the therapist can help clients marshall their own resources while resolving their conflicting feelings about proceeding. Families should be unanimously sure that the risks are worth it before they undertake an intervention. Not uncommonly, one or more family members will express concern about suicide in these early meetings; although I have never heard of a suicide following an intervention, I do not discount or minimize these concerns. Therapists who are too eager or pushy are more likely to precipitate a potentially destructive process, leaving family members regretting having done the intervention.

(2) Alcoholism Education

In order to help family members approach the alcoholic in a loving manner, as opposed to being rejecting and hostile, it is essential that they understand that the alcoholic is trapped inside of the disease and desperately needs outside help in order to change. Most families are either resentful and bitter or intimidated and guilty. Since they do not understand that the drinker is out of control, they take his/her actions in a reactive and personal way, e.g., "If he loved me, he wouldn't behave like that." I urge the family to think of the alcoholic as one might think of an Alzheimer's patient who is slowly losing his/her mind, ability to relate in the world coherently, and capability to reverse the process. The difference is that Alzheimer's patients can never recover, while alcoholics, if they get appropriate help, can regain their life and their relationships. I also point out that the drinkers' resistance to treatment does not mean that they do not want any help. It often means that they think they cannot be treated and cannot live without dependency on chemicals.

By emphasizing the alcoholic's helplessness and desperate need for outside support, I am attempting to counter the accumulation of negative and hostile feelings that are perfectly normal for those people who have been on the receiving end of an alcoholic's behavior. I encourage family members to acknowledge their feelings of rage, bitterness, fear, and hopelessness and then help them to understand that those very feelings become ensnared with the alcoholic's defenses and denial. For example, the wife who is legitimately enraged by her husband's behavior inadvertently becomes part of the rationalizations that he uses to justify drinking, e.g., "I wouldn't drink so much if she wasn't bitchin' at me all the time." Using the disease concept is the most effective way of building an empathic bridge between the family and the alcoholic, "the person trapped inside the bottle."

(3) Preparing Data and Formulating the Treatment Plan

The heart of an intervention is when the group gives very concrete and specific feedback to the alcoholic about the impact of his/her drinking on his/her behavior, health and relationship to others. The group is taught how to give examples of situations and behaviors that relate to drinking without being blaming or judgmental. The assumption is that the alcoholic cannot see what other people can see. The catalytic effect of the intervention is in part created by the accumulation of facts that demonstrate the pervasive and destructive pattern of abuse. Rationalizing an individual episode of drinking is relatively easy; explaining a way the whole pattern over an extended time involving all aspects of a drinker's life is not. The daughter's confronting her mother about finding her drinking early on a Thanksgiving morning is powerful not only in itself but also because it is one of 50 similiar descriptions.

These painful facts must be presented in the context of love, concern, and desire for the drinker to face the problem and to seek treatment, as stated by each member of the group. The leader of the intervention needs to help people express their positions without being attacking and blaming. It is useful to have participants actually write out their statements, so that they can clearly see and delete expressions of antagonism and judgment.

In addition to preparing statements, the participants need to develop a consensus about what kind of treatment they will ask the drinker to accept. The standard plan is for the alcoholic to enter a 30-day inpatient treatment program. Although inpatient treatment may not be significantly more successful than outpatient, this is an easy way to capitalize on the momentum of the intervention process. Quitting drinking on an outpatient basis takes a tremendous amount of dedication. A drinker who goes through an intervention, will tend initially to be motivated by the external concern and pressure from the group rather than by internal goals; the desire to quit drinking has not had time to build. An inpatient setting often gives clients time to develop their own motivation to overcome the addiction.

If the group is going to push for an inpatient program, the logistical problems of arranging bed space, time off from work, family availability for participation, and financing are all worked out in advance. While it is a harsh shock for the alcoholic to have to go through an intervention, it is the enormity of taking a month off from work that is most difficult for many. If the intervention group has prepared carefully, the alcoholic will simply have less to worry about and fewer excuses not to go. The hospital chosen should have staff comfortable with the intervention technique and a well-developed plan for family treatment. St. Mary's Hospital in Minneapolis is renowned for their week-long family program, which has become a model for many treatment centers around the country. This kind of program provides a follow-up of the intervention and an opportunity for the drinker and the family to be reunited with the acknowledgment that everyone in the family needs to work on recovery.

Although family members will usually propose an inpatient program, they need to have a backup choice if the drinker is adamantly opposed to going away for a month. The critical part of an intervention is not getting the drinker off to treatment. Rather, it is helping the drinker genuinely acknowledge the seriousness of the problem and express a willingness to change. If the alcoholic has not attempted to stop or control drinking in the past, then his/her response to the intervention may be to accept the feedback but insist on the right to handle the problem. The family needs to be able to negotiate some kind of mutually acceptable plan with the drinker without polarizing the situation. I usually coach families to

first push for their treatment plan. If they meet rigid and unyielding resistance, then they should accept the drinker's plan with the
agreement that if he/she does not succeed with that plan then the
family's approach will be tried.

When the alcoholic insists on trying his/her own approach, the
likelihood of success is slim. The intervention group needs to be
prepared for this outcome and willing to confront the alcoholic
again. In this second intervention I expect the group to take tough
and unyielding action vis-à-vis the drinker. The group has to be
willing to set clear limits, such as, "We gave you an opportunity to
stop drinking on your own. If you continue to drink, I will have to
move out of the house," or "I am afraid that we will no longer be
able to have you working for us if you continue to be unwillling to
seek treatment." Motivating the group for this second intervention
is difficult, since people feel defeated and discouraged. After their
dedication and hard work, they feel right back where they started.
Helping the group understand the possible necessity of a second
intervention, which may be much more difficult than the first, is a
significant component of the overall preparation sessions.

(4) The Rehearsal

During the rehearsal the participants organize the order of their
presentations, edit their written statements, anticipate the alcoholic's potential attempts to sabotage the meeting, and basically help
each other overcome their stage fright. The group actually prac-
tices the whole intervention, making the presentation to an empty
chair.

The group chooses a leader who will introduce the whole process to the drinker and gently and politely ask him/her to allow the
participants to make their presentation without interruption. The
leader should be someone who has the complete respect of the
drinker and will be supportively firm in helping the drinker sit
through the process. If the drinker does become obsteperous, then
the leader is the one who helps him/her regain composure. The
group is carefully coached not to engage in fighting with the drinker. In one case, the leader simply had to inform the argumentative
drinker that the group was prepared to wait in silence for as necessary until the drinker was ready to listen. The group leader, along
with the therapist, assumes primary responsibility for moderating

the meeting and particularly for keeping the discussion focused and not argumentative during the latter part, when treatment plans are being discussed.

We pay special attention to the actual order of presentations, since it is likely that different people will have considerably different levels of impact. The wife who has been heard on the subject ad nauseum will tend to have much less impact than the best friend who has never mentioned the problem before. Participants who are likely to have a negative impact are sandwiched between the people whom the drinker will be able to hear and respect. It adds power to have the most significant speakers come at the end of the meeting. For example, the little girl who spoke to her grandmother was the second to last in the whole group; by the time the meeting came around to her, grandmother had heard an accumulation of feelings, worries, declarations of love, and the facts. She was no longer able to block out her granddaughter's love, fear, and concern.

Also during the rehearsal, the participants rework their statements to remove any lingering implications of blame and hostility. There is a obvious difference between "You wrecked our kids' lives because you were always drunk!" and "I remember when you missed all of John's Little League games because you didn't get home on time. You would go to the bar instead. You were a wonderful father but I feel your drinking caused you to miss out on a lot of the kids' growing-up years."

Finally, the rehearsal enables the participants to become more comfortable with intensity of their feelings. Usually several people are quite tearful and overwhelmed. The group is able to take the time to support and encourage them. The members come away with an enhanced sense of the importance of what they are doing as well as an appreciation of their own strength. As this happens I move out of the center. Interventions work when the group becomes cohesive and able to take care of its members with little help from me.

(5) The Intervention

Regardless of whether the intervention is successful, the attempt on the part of the people who love the drinker to reach through the walls of denial to the person trapped within is quite moving. If the group is well prepared and large enough to somewhat overwhelm

the drinker, then the session does not become explosive or turn
into a free-for-all. Instead it is quiet, intense, and sad.

I remember a withdrawn, surly teenage girl who had been hostile and uncooperative throughout the preparation. I had wondered
if she should even be invited to the intervention, since she seemed
so harshly angry. She had refused to say anything at the rehearsal
but insisted that she would be ready to talk when the time came.
When it was her turn, she just sat and said nothing. After a long
wait her chest began to heave as she fought back the tears. Finally
she read to her father, "I remember when I was 11 years old, you
. . . you were so drunk that you went into the bathroom and threw
up. I remember lying in bed and listening to you. Then instead of
going back into your room you made a wrong turn and came
stumbling into my bedroom. You were naked and you didn't even
know where you were. You got on the bed next to me. You turned
to me and put your leg over me. I couldn't move. After a while you
began to snore. I pulled myself away from you and went and sat in
the corner. I sat in the corner all night. I was so embarrassed. I am
supposed to tell you how much I love you and everything but I
can't. I just want you to stop drinking. I want to have a father
again. That's all I've got to say."

Nobody spoke. Nobody looked at the father. The girl crumpled
up her piece of paper and dropped it on the floor.

Interventions usually have one of three relatively predictable outcomes. About half the time the drinker lets go of his defenses and
accepts the group and the suggestions. In those cases, the general
tone is one of profound relief and even joy. There are hugs all
around as the drinker and the family seem to be reunited by the
experience and the emerging sense of hope.

About a third of the time the drinker accepts the legitimacy of
the feedback and acknowledges the seriousness of the problem but
rejects the notion of inpatient treatment. When the group retreats
to the backup option, the drinker is often so relieved that he/she
readily agrees to try inpatient treatment later if his/her own plan
does not work. The group has to be prepared for the likelihood
that it will take a second, tougher intervention to make the drinker
keep his commitment.

In less than 20 percent of the cases, the drinker refuses help,
denies the problem, or attempts to fight with the group. The participants are prepared for this eventuality and have spent some time

in the planning stages considering how they will relate to the alcoholic if he continues to drink and refuses any kind of treatment. Usually most people in the group simply state that they will withdraw actively from the relationship while continuing to hope that the drinker will see the light. This response is not considered a threat. Instead it is a sad and painful acknowledgment that continuing to relate to an alcoholic who will not seek treatment means becoming part of the problem rather than part of the solution. It is unfortunately true that many alcoholics do not get the message until it smacks them in the face and that frequently means the loss of those people closest to them. Two of my interventions did not work until the wife was willing to pack up herself and the children and move out. In one the family was reunited later in sobriety; in the other the husband has been sober for five years but he and his wife, after a long separation, are now getting a divorce.

(6) Follow-up

There should always be a follow-up session after an intervention, regardless of whether it went well or badly. Participating in one of these procedures is emotionally draining and overwhelming, and having the opportunity to meet again is often essential in terms of bringing some kind of closure to the experience. The follow-up may be a kind of family celebration in which the drinker and group discuss their experiences in the recovery process, or it may be a second intervention in which the drinker is urged to try the group's plan, or it may be a postmortem in which the participants support one another in their pain as they acknowledge that the intervention did not work and nothing more can be done. In any case, the follow-up enables the therapist to help the participants support each other in feeling positively about the experience regardless of the outcome, to identify members who need some ongoing help, and to educate the group about some of the difficulties that usually ensue once a family is in recovery.

How Many Sessions Does It Usually Take to Do an Intervention?

The number of sessions varies, depending on the level of sophistication of the participants and their unanimity about wanting to do an intervention. I have done some interventions over a very intense weekend, meeting with family and friends all day Saturday and doing the intervention itself on Sunday. On the other hand, one intervention I did required several meetings over six months because of the difficulties involved in building an effective, united group.

Generally, preparation takes about six to eight hours and the intervention itself lasts about an hour. It is almost never wrong to go slowly. I would rather risk losing a group than push people into an intervention before they are ready.

IS IT USEFUL TO DO AN INTERVENTION EVEN IF YOU CANNOT INVOLVE A LARGE NETWORK OF PEOPLE?

Many times it is difficult to engage a large group. I am currently working on a case in which the family of a prominent lawyer is seeking to do an intervention. After meeting with them, I realize that the lawyer has managed to control his alcoholism, so that only immediate family members really know how serious the problem is. If people from the lawyer's work life or extended family were brought in, they would probably not be able to confront him in a useful way, since they do not have the firsthand experience with his drinking being a difficulty. We will go ahead and do the intervention anyway because it is important for the family members' sake that they take a stand on the alcoholism in a loving and supportive way, even though they have to do it alone. Interventions are as much a healing process for the participants as for the drinker. Regardless of the outcome, the intervention participants will feel that they have made their best effort to reach out to the alcoholic.

If the intervention group is not representative of a significant cross section of a person's life, then its chances for success are reduced. Alcoholics are very skilled at resisting any one pressure point, whether it's work, family, or friends. It's the combination of all three that is usually most potent. However, families often have to decide whether going behind the alcoholic's back in order to engage people at work or significant others may cause the alcoholic to feel irrevocably betrayed. Families have to decide between compromising with the alcoholic and creating an intervention group that will have maximum impact.

Jack was an alcoholic who came to the early sessions and adamantly refused to have his business partner involved. He said that he would leave the family if they invited his partner. I encouraged the family to back down on the issue, because I was working hard on helping him accept the idea of the intervention. The intervention, ultimately held with only the immediate family members, was unsuccessful. In retrospect it is clear that I undercut the family members by letting the alcoholic have too much control. I should have encouraged them to go ahead and talk to the drinker's friends and business partners despite his opposition. Now it is five years later and Jack is still drinking, his partners have given up on him, his marriage is gone, and his health is rapidly going. On the other hand, his ex-wife and his four children have successfully moved on in their lives and feel that the intervention freed them from being dominated by the alcoholic. They can say, "At least we did the best we could."

CAN YOU USE THE INTERVENTION TECHNIQUE WITH OTHER MENTAL HEALTH PROBLEMS BESIDES ALCOHOLISM?

Once I became comfortable with the concept of interventions, I felt I could adapt the method to fit different family circumstances. It seemed that this approach might work in other family situations in which someone was in serious trouble and unwilling either to acknowledge the problem or to seek treatment. Although I have not used the technique on a wide variety of cases, I feel it can be used with families with a depressed or mentally ill member, families with a chronically sick member who is not taking care of him/herself, or families of people with eating disorders or other psychosomatic disorders.

Recently I have done a modified intervention on a family with an anorectic member. It was extremely powerful in helping break through her denial about the seriousness of her problem. She has now accepted what she needs for treatment and training to learn how to put on weight. The emphasis in the intervention approach on expressing love and concern rather than blame and hostility allowed these highly enmeshed, conflict-avoiding family members to feel supportive and loyal to the anorectic while confronting her.

For twenty years Albert has been a brittle diabetic who routinely was irresponsible about managing his diet. The result has been that he would go into insulin shock. When he goes into shock, he has seizures, becomes violent, and passes out. If he is not treated immediately he will die. He has been rushed to the hospital over one hundred times by his overfunctioning wife, who is, naturally, the adult child of an alcoholic. Both his doctor and his wife have repeatedly confronted him with the need for him to take better care of himself and with the magnitude of the burden his disease puts on the whole family. In a modified intervention, his 12-year-old daughter carefully described her feelings of fear and helplessness as she tried to give him a shot while he was rolling around on the floor in the middle of a seizure. His eyes filled with tears. He looked down at his hands and whispered, "I didn't know. I just didn't know."

In chess, the endgame is the last stage of the match, when many of the pieces have been lost and the players are down to the final maneuvers—going for a checkmate or fending off a checkmate. Sometimes the aggressor wins. Sometimes the defender staves off defeat and forces a draw. In any case, the game ends.

An intervention is an endgame maneuver. It breaks the pattern. Drinkers do not necessarily stop drinking. They do not always go into hospitals. Families do not always follow through on their commitments to disengage from the drinker or go into treatment themselves. Sometimes it looks like nothing has changed. Sometimes the whole family seems transformed and a chain of addiction linking generations is broken. But win, lose, or draw, the game ends. After an intervention, the participants cannot easily continue to play their old roles. It is harder to enable, it is harder to pursue, and it is harder to drink. One recovering alcoholic, who had been through an intervention but didn't quit until some years after, said, "It didn't stop me from drinking but it sure did take all of the fun out of it."

I do interventions because they work and because I know that even when they do not work they still help families break the bonds of guilt, responsibility, shame, and anger tying them to alcoholism. I do interventions because I believe that locked inside of an alcoholic there is a drowning person who is flailing about in panic and who wants to be rescued. One man summed it up when he said, "It goes without saying that it saved my life. But what sticks out in my mind is — I couldn't believe that they cared so much, that they still loved me. I will never forget that."

5

The Many Mornings After: Couples Therapy, Part Three

Ann sits bolt upright on the edge of the chair with her hands folded in her lap and her knees pressed tightly together. She is dressed in her Sunday best. Her hair is carefully coiffed and her makeup impeccable. The smile on her face seems to be as carefully put on as her lipstick. She does not glance at her husband as she says to me, "I'm so glad that Bill is home from the program. He seems so much better to me. I'm really very proud of him. The children are proud of him too. We all know how hard he's trying and we are prepared to do anything to help him."

Bill can't sit still in his seat. He keeps shifting his position and his hands are fidgeting. Bill is smiling. His eyes dart furtively in Ann's direction as he says to me, "Things will be really different now that I'm in the program. I feel better than I have in years. I couldn't have done it without Ann and the kids. I'm just glad to have another chance. We've got a lot of time to make up for."

The two kids look terrified. When asked how they feel about Dad's coming home from the hospital they both say that they are very happy that their Dad is well now.

The morning after the storm, you have a sense of relief. You can't resist pouring over the charts and eagerly measuring the distance to port. Slowly it dawns on you, there are many miles to go. There will be more storms and more calms. In the warm sunshine, the momentary relief fades. It is not over. It is still a long way home. There are many mornings after.

Early recovery is a tense time. Everyone is on best behavior. Everyone is scared that the sobriety will not last. No one knows quite how to relate to each other. It is like trying to run a car engine without the lubricating oil. All the parts grind on each other.

Inside the family members, tremendous hurt, anxiety, and rage have been bottled up during years of dealing with the substance abuse; yet the situation calls for them to plaster smiles on their faces and to act like they are thrilled with their newly sober member. On the other hand, the alcoholic has to discover that the family really has learned to get along without him or her and that he is truly an outsider in his own home. Furthermore, as he becomes aware of the destructiveness of his past behavior, he realizes there is absolutely no way of making up for it. His level of shame and need for forgiveness is extremely high, at the same time that the family's ability to genuinely forgive and accept is extremely low. This period of adjustment is so traumatic for families that many of them break up. Others develop a symptom bearer whose behavior allows the family to maintain its familiar crisis-oriented structure. Others simply return to the substance abuse and all the old patterns associated with it. The paradox of recovery is that often everyone in the family feels worse while expecting to feel so much better. The famous "pink cloud" carries acid rain.

Efforts to improve relationships at a time of peak vulnerability set these families up for a return to drinking behavior. Therefore, it is very important at this stage of treatment for the therapist to initiate a restraint-from-change intervention. Following are some samples of the messages I want to get across to family members.

To the recovering alcoholic: "Don't try and make up for the past. It won't work. Your spouse and children are trying hard to let you in, but in reality they have so much buried resentment against you that they really can't let you in. If you try to move in too quickly, you will just be putting pressure on them to resolve their feelings before they are ready to. Give them time. When you are feeling those periods of being a stranger inside your family, use AA."

To the spouse: "I know you think you're supposed to be able to welcome this guy back with open arms. However, I think that you're trying too hard is very hurtful to him and his recovery. He'll sense the part of you that is still locked away, the part of you that can't trust him and can't forgive him and that maybe doesn't even want to recommit to this relationship. You can't will away the scars of the last few years any more than he could conquer drinking with willpower. You survived by learning how to get along without him. The minute you try to let him into the family and begin to share some control, your hurt and bitterness will become overwhelming. Don't force it. Let him work his program while you work yours. Use Al-Anon. They will help you appreciate that you need time for healing also."

To the children: "You know your Dad would desperately like to make up for the time he lost with you. He's missed a lot of your growing up years. But I don't want him to try and come on like Super Dad because that will only put tremendous pressure on you. Don't be afraid of your resentment and mistrust. If you didn't have these feelings somewhere inside you, you wouldn't be normal. Lots of kids are so afraid that their Dad will go back to drinking that they don't know what to do with the feelings of anger that well up inside. I have a good friend who has been sober about ten years. When her daughter was a senior in high school a couple of years ago, she wrote a story about her mother's alcoholism. In the last part of the story she tells how, whenever she is going over to her mother's house for a visit, she finds herself carefully avoiding stepping on the cracks in the sidewalk, lest she find her mother drunk again. Eight years into sobriety, the fear remains. It takes a long time."

After preparing all the family members for the tension of the early recovery period and restraining them from attempting too much change, I push hard for a commitment to AA, Al-Anon, and Al-Ateen. If the children are in good shape, I continue the work primarily with the couple. If the children begin to get into trouble as a way of substituting themselves for the alcohol game, then I bring them into the therapy without hesitation. Even when the children are doing well, there are several points in the couples treatment when it is useful to involve them.

The heart of preparing a couple and a family for the difficulties and disappointments of recovery is to encourage each person to focus on themselves and reduce their expectations for change in their relationships with each other. Unlike traditional therapy, clients are taught how to live with difficult feelings rather than attempt to resolve them. The stages of the therapy are carefully choreographed so that family members can make the journey to recovery one step at a time. In Chapter 3 we discussed the Disengagement stage of treatment when the substance abuse is still active. The following five stages take place once a couple has made a committment to recovery.

Stage 2: Differentiation

Hypotheses

My first hypothesis is: *The couple that has been organized around a pattern of substance abuse will be profoundly destabilized by sobriety.* The spouses will be like strangers to each other without their familiar, although painful, pattern.

The second hypothesis is: *Couples in recovery generally have very exaggerated expectations of what sobriety is supposed to accomplish.* Spouses who have not experienced much genuine intimacy throughout an extended period of their marriage expect that with the onset of sobriety they should suddenly develop closeness. Frequently these expectations create considerable pressure.

The third hypothesis is: *Tensions around the changes in patterned behavior are so great that relapses frequently happen as a way of returning to normal.* Therefore, it is appropriate for the therapist to be prepared for a return to drinking behavior, without being intimidated by this possibility. Sometimes people drink in the first year of sobriety as a way of truly discovering on their own that they can't drink. This is particularly true of those people who feel that they were somehow forced to give up drinking.

The last hypothesis is: *The spouses become more deeply in touch with the awful dimensions of emotional hurt and lost time that they have experienced during the struggles around the sub-*

stance abuse. In the heat of battle soldiers do not experience their feelings; the shock does not wear off until the shooting stops. The effect is very similiar for the couple in early recovery. With the end of the crisis and the beginning of sobriety comes an overwhelming-ly painful awareness of what the substance abuse wars have really done to both partners. Therefore, it is reasonable to expect that one or both will experience significant depression in the earlier stages of recovery.

Goals

The primary goal in early recovery is simply to help the family tolerate discomfort and confusion with sobriety and to reduce ex-pectations about early recovery.

Since the spouses are on such unfamiliar territory, I encourage them to maintain their old pattern of relationship while removing the substance use. If this particular pattern has involved a husband and wife frequently separated, with the husband off at a bar, then the goal will be to maintain a similar level of separation, with the husband perhaps at an AA meeting instead of a bar. Similarly, if the spouses have been sexually or emotionally distant, I do not want them to attempt to close the gap that has been exposed by the removal of alcohol. Restraining them from working on their rela-tionship during early recovery is protective. The changes brought by sobriety are hard enough to handle without the risks involved in attempting to resolve all the old issues around closeness and intimacy.

Strategies

The strategies of the differentiation stage are all restraint-from-change interventions. It is important to note before discussing these strategies that I am not using a paradoxical approach in the hopes of causing people to get closer and more intimate. I want them to literally resist working on intimacy issues during the early stages of recovery. There are three basic strategies that I use during the differentiation stage: education, structure, and discussion of "the car ride home."

Education about the disease model. I do a considerable amount of reframing of the couple's history as being the product of the disease of alcoholism and its related pattern in the family system. Whenever possible I use the disease model as a means of scape-goating the alcohol in a way that diffuses some of the intensity of the fault finding and the mutual recrimination. I also emphasize the disease model as a way of motivating the couple to use AA and Al-Anon. Therapy is secondary in importance to working the Program. Thirdly, I normalize the feelings of rage, despair, depression, anxiety, resentment, bitterness, etc. I want the spouses to understand why they have these difficult feelings without feeling pressure to resolve them.

Structure of the therapy. Couples in the turmoil of early recovery often need the security that comes from understanding the treatment plan. I describe the therapy in quite specific terms and discuss the organization of the different stages. I also organize the therapy hour by dividing the session in half. Each spouse is given a half hour to work with me on learning more effective coping skills and dealing with the practical difficulties of everyday life. I do not let the other spouse interrupt and I block the individual with whom I am talking from attacking the spouse. This breaks the pattern of mutual recrimination and fosters each person's taking individual responsibility. Rather than focusing on relationship issues, I ask each spouse to work on issues that are not dependent on the other's support or participation. The emphasis is on addressing here-and-now problems rather than the painful past. Frequently I refer to the past as a dangerous monster that will have to be let out of its cage and struggled with sooner or later, but at this point they should concentrate on building up the strength necessary to make that struggle successful.

As I work with each individual in the presence of the other, the therapy has a significant effect on the couple relationship. It may be the first time in years that either has actually sat and listened to the other one talk. This particular strategy begins to break up the fusion which is almost always inherent in alcoholic couple systems and enables each spouse to understand and have more empathy for the other.

The car ride home. Clearly these highly controlled sessions are difficult for the couple to manage emotionally. I usually close the session with comments about "the car ride home" and the likelihood that the spouses will tear into each other once they are out of the office. She might say, "I can't believe that you implied that you have always been involved with the kids when you haven't been home sober for ten years!" He might say, "It's really great that you get to make it sound like everything is my fault. I wasn't always a drunk, but you were always a bitch!" I ask couples not to talk about the meeting and to avoid using what each other has said as a weapon. I want the office to be a safe place. In anticipating the car ride home, I discuss how they will handle their stirred-up feelings so that they can sidestep a conflict. With particularly volatile and reactive couples, I encourage them to keep a private journal of their hostile and blaming feelings, so that they have some means of discharging their built-up frustration.

My experience with these couples has taught me that my making these rules is frequently no more successful than the effort of the English King, Canute, who went with his entire retinue down to the beach in order to demonstrate that he could command the tide not to come in. He ended up all wet. Helping these spouses learn to be less reactive to each other and more responsible for themselves is a process that they slowly learn rather than something that the therapist commands.

Outcome

Generally a successful outcome of this stage is indicated when the couple is able to tolerate the restraint from change and each individual is able to focus attention on his or her own recovery. The couple should be using AA and Al-Anon and living by the philosophy of "one day at a time." Another manifestation of a successful outcome is the couple's report of less conflict and tension at home. This kind of progress is usually an indication that the couple is ready to move on to the next stage.

A second outcome is that the couple basically drops out of therapy, but without returning to drinking or giving up AA or Al-Anon. Although it sometimes takes me by surprise, this particular outcome is an indicator that the spouses have their own internal wisdom about the pacing of their recovery and are taking my restraint-from-change suggestions to heart.

The third outcome occurs when the couple actively coalesces against the therapist. Having been restrained from attacking each other in such a dominating manner by me, the couple may join forces and attack me. I need to accept the attack and positively connote their wisdom in attacking me rather than each other. It is important for me to be comfortable with their frustrations and encourage them to express these feelings whenever they are experiencing too much distress. Sometimes couples will respond to restraint-from-change suggestions by colluding to work on closeness and intimacy in spite of my warnings. I have learned not to get too enthusiastic about the occasional paradoxical effect of these "go slow" interventions and to maintain a conservative stance around the risk of changing too quickly.

Another outcome is that the substance abuser begins to have relapses. If I can avoid overreacting to the relapse, I usually can help the alcoholic and the spouse deal with the slip effectively. My assumption is that the return to active substance abuse is an indication that the anxiety level of the system has gone beyond what the couple can tolerate without resort to the old abuse pattern. I remember my surprise when I first heard a wife report that there was much less tension in the family now that her husband had started to drink again. I have subsequently learned that the fastest way for an alcoholic system to reduce its level of tension and discomfort is to have a return to drinking.

I discuss openly with the couple the possibility that a slip may happen and encourage the drinker and spouse not to panic if it does. Slips are defined as meaning that we have been moving too fast and that it's time to get back to the basics of early recovery and the use of support programs. Obviously, if slips continue to happen, there is something seriously flawed in the therapy. The therapist should consider consulting with another therapist to review what is enabling the on-and-off relapses. The therapy itself may have become part of the problem. It might be necessary to recommend inpatient treatment or a return to the basic disengagement strategies used in the first stage (see Chapter 3).

STAGE 3: NEGOTIATION

Hypothesis

Usually spouses have a difficult time working cooperatively together and functioning as a mutually respectful team. In most cases there has been a strong hierarchical skew in which the spouse has been the overfunctioner and the substance abuser has been treated more like a difficult child than a partner.

Goals

I want to teach the marital partners negotiating and problem-solving skills that will enhance their sense of competence and their ability to work together. Negotiating techniques help them interrupt their typically adversarial pattern as well as develop appropriate expectations of each other. My goal is to teach them how to subordinate their feelings in order to work effectively together. I also want to create a line of demarcation between their history of mutual failure and recrimination and the present effort at teamwork and cooperation.

Strategies

Working with present issues. In order to help the couple learn negotiating skills it is useful to begin with issues that are relatively minor and nonthreatening. We focus on present situations without bringing up references to past struggles. I explain that the purpose of this stage is to lay down a new pattern of cooperation and compromise. Typical issues that might be negotiated are: what the spouses are going to do over the weekend, how they are going to talk to the children about Dad's or Mom's recovery, and what kind of rules they should follow telling friends and relatives about the drinking situation. No issues are particularly easy. In addition, it is important that they understand that any issue they pick to work on may have deep roots in conflicts and feelings from the past.

Therapist as arbitrator. Taking on the role of an arbitrator, the therapist pushes the couple towards making agreements and compromises. As the therapist directs the spouses to engage each other in dialogue, they will usually resort to old patterns of blaming and mutual disrespect. The therapist intervenes in the flow of the interview in order to keep the couple focused on the task of coming up with some resolution to the issue at hand. The following is a brief example of the kind of interaction that one would expect to have between the therapist and both spouses.

JOHN   Well, you never have let me get involved in balancing the checkbook before.

D.T.   Hold it John, don't start bringing up the past here. Just see if Ruth is interested in working with you on the checkbook now.

RUTH   Well, I don't see how I can let him do that because he doesn't have a clue as to what the household expenses are.

D.T.   Well, Ruth, what you need to think about is whether or not letting John work with you on the checkbook would be a way to help him know where the money goes.

JOHN   I don't think she wants to have me find out where the money goes. I think she wants to keep control of everything.

D.T.   Okay, you guys, before we go any further let's get back to working out a deal. Start over again, John, and tell Ruth what you'd like to do with the checkbook.

Obviously, I am engaged in a very directive style of therapy. If the spouses are left on their own, these discussions degenerate into reactive blaming quite quickly.

Preparing for the letdown effect. When couples finally succeed at making compromises and working together, normally they experience a letdown. After all, they may have been struggling with each other for 20 years; when they begin to work together, it usually stirs up all the old feelings of frustration and disappointment. Ironically, in this stage success may feel to one or both spouses like "too little and too late."

At first I was taken aback by this letdown effect and would attempt to cheerlead the partners about their accomplishments. Now I prepare them for the likelihood that they will not feel great after making some progress. I describe how others have been surprised that accomplishing these negotiations has often stirred up old hurtful and angry feelings. I tell about the wife who blurted out at the end of one of these negotiation sessions, "You mean I have been waiting 25 years for him to agree that he should take out the garbage once a week? Big deal!"

Maintaining the old structure. While the spouses are learning negotiating skills, I generally encourage them to maintain their old hierarchical structure. It is a big step for them to be engaged in negotiating in the first place; it takes a long time for them to reorganize the hierarchy. "Running things" may be the only way that the co-dependent has felt safe both in the marriage and in her own childhood. If they now want to negotiate about parenting, it is not helpful either to expect the co-dependent to give up her position of being in charge of the children or to encourage the alcoholic to step into an active coparenting role. All family members have become dependent on the roles they have played during the years of active substance abuse; it is important not to push them to give up old roles precipitously.

This particular message is important for the recovering person, who often feels very left out and disempowered in the family. I might say to him, "You have every right to want Jack to let you make decisions with him about the boys, but at this point you need to understand that he's not able to let you in. He's been handling the boys for a long time pretty much like a single parent and it will be very hard for him to learn how to share control with you."

While I encourage the couple to maintain the old structure, usually with the co-dependent parent left in charge, I do begin to empower the recovering parent vis-à-vis the children by urging him/her to educate them about alcoholism as a disease, the purpose of AA, Al-Anon and Al-Ateen and the slowness of the recovery process. I want the recovering parent to be in charge of helping the kids accept their own anxieties and distrust about whether he/she really will recover. I ask him/her to explain to the kids that their first priority is to concentrate on sobriety and that for the time being it is best for the other parent to stay in charge. This kind of negotiated cease-fire allows the parents to cooperate without trying to change their respective roles too much just yet.

Outcome

Usually the spouses begin to experience some sense of accomplishment and enhanced ability to work together. Although the "letdown effect" happens no matter how carefully I prepare them, most clients still feel increased self-confidence and trust as they discover that they can make deals and carry them out.

Sometimes seemingly benign and relatively easy issues become impossible to control once the couple begins negotiating. Just because I have a plan and a structure does not mean that I am really in control of the therapeutic process. If the partners escalate into unmanageable conflict, then I usually suggest that we move backward to the differentiation stage until they feel better prepared to work together. For example, a wife may be highly reluctant to work out any agreements with her husband whatsoever. Her level of distrust may be so high that she needs to work separately on her own issues before doing business with him. When clients are struggling with the therapy model, I see it as information and assume that the model needs to be adjusted to fit the particular clients.

If the negotiation effort leads to an outbreak of drinking, the most obvious thing to do is to step back to an earlier stage in the recovery process. As at other stages, I treat the "slip" as an indication that we may be going too fast or overlooking something in the therapy. I want to avoid the toxicity of either spouse blaming him/ herself or the other. Treating the slip simply as a signal to move backwards a little seems to take some of the sting out of it. (What I like best about this particular treatment model is that it is the only one I know of with a reverse gear.)

The main questions that I use to assess whether the couple is ready for the next stage are:

- Is the couple carrying out the tasks at home?
- Are the spouses tolerating each other's discouragement and sense of frustration about the arbitration process?
- Do the spouses spontaneously begin to work together more cooperatively and independently?
- Is the couple beginning to chafe at the bit about the degree of

therapeutic control and the relative insignificance of the issues being negotiated?

STAGE 4: CONFLICT MANAGEMENT

Hypotheses

The primary hypothesis is that chemical abuse has been a significant element in the couple's pattern of dealing with conflict. For some couples chemical use is a way to interrupt a fighting sequence. The fight ends when he stomps out the door to have a drink. In the past, it may have been that the fight was necessary for the drinker, in order to give him a just cause for going off to drink. On the other hand, substance use on the part of one or both spouses may have reduced inhibitions and intensified the conflict. For some couples substance use dampens tension and anger; for others it ignites it. There is almost always a direct link between the pattern of substance abuse and the couple's ways of handling conflict.

Couples in early recovery are tense and confused about how to handle conflict. Generally spouses attempt to avoid open conflict at all costs because of the underlying fear that fighting will lead to drinking. At the same time, they are also experiencing all the normal discomfort of not knowing how to live together and what to expect from each other. Conflict is normal, but frightening, during this stage.

Finally, I assume that there is a considerable residue of hurt and anger. Spouses avoid triggering past resentments, fearing an escalation in which they do irretrievable damage to each other. Such conflict-avoidant behavior can be seen as a mutual nonaggression pact, in which the wife spares the husband all that she might say about what a disaster he was during his drinking years and the husband spares the wife the accusation that it was her fault that he drank in the first place.

Goals

The spouses need to learn how to tolerate conflict and its aftermath, how to fight fairly without resorting to "below the belt" tactics, and how to tolerate unresolved conflict without allowing it to escalate out of control.

Strategies

Practicing unresolved conflict. Framing this stage of treatment as "practicing conflict" is very important since the spouses need to feel safe about addressing their issues around fighting. I make it clear that moving into the conflict management stage is a manifestation of their significant progress and that the learning how to tolerate unresolved conflict is the goal.

In the office, I have them them take turns presenting arguments for 15 minutes; then, at the half-hour mark, they stop and I talk to each of them individually about how they are going to handle their stirred-up feelings without escalating the fight. Frequently, what emerges is that each person is feeling quite vulnerable. Some of the hostile behavior can be reframed as a manifestation of this vulnerability and fear. I also ask whether either spouse is concerned that this particular fight may lead to a drinking episode. Since this concern is almost always present but unspoken, my discussing it directly and openly usually has a detoxifying effect.

Fair fighting rules. Having set up a structure for the conflict, I then encourage the partners to follow a series of interactional rules designed to provide them with a feeling of safety and control. The rules are as follows:

(1) The couple is enjoined from referring to past behavior when having a conflict in the present. While the spouses are learning to manage conflict and to tolerate disagreements, bringing up the past as a weapon is not acceptable. Phrases beginning with "You never . . . " or "You always . . . " are discouraged.

(2) The couple must stay on the mutually agreed-upon topic. Neither individual is allowed to "rolodex" the fights (that is, switch from a losing position to a new topic, e.g. "Well, maybe you did take out the trash but you still forgot my birthday").

(3) Either spouse is allowed to withdraw from a fight at any time if he/she senses that things are getting out of hand. This protects the couple from potentially negative consequences. It is the withdrawer's responsibility to negotiate a time for

reconvening on the issue. When this rule is followed, the partner knows that withdrawal will not be used as a way to avoid dealing with issues entirely.

Homework. In addition to the work in the office, the couple must practice these conflict management skills at home. I frequently ask spouses to schedule, at home between sessions, two or three conflicts that cannot be resolved. They are to disengage at a set time, going off to separate meetings or activities in the house, and to keep track of their feelings during one of these staged conflicts in a diary. I also prescibe occasional "cheap shots" to enable the couple to practice avoiding unplanned fights. Each spouse lists his/her partner's most provocative comments. Then the partner is instructed to say those things in the course of the week, so that the recipient of the barb can learn to avoid taking the hook.

Clearly, all these techniques have to be adjusted to fit the couple's particular style. I usually give clients a considerable latitude in choosing the homework assignment that fits them the best.

Outcome

Conflict and management strategies lead to a variety of different outcomes. When couples are able to learn rules of fair fighting and can tolerate the open conflict, they feel a positive sense of emerging competency and mastery mingled with a sense of sadness about how much pain they have endured over the years. This particular reaction foreshadows the work in the next stage, resolution of the past, as individuals become emotionally in touch with their pain once they emerge from a perpetual state of conflict.

Some couples will not be able to handle the conflict. With them the therapist needs to gently release the pressure to continue in the stage and to encourage them to go back to a much more controlled, walking-on-eggshells, working-their-separate-programs approach. The difficulty of managing conflict must be appreciated.

Drinking is more likely to happen during this stage than during any of the preceding ones. A drinking episode is a signal to retreat to individual issues and working the program rather than continuing to pursue open conflicts.

Some couples persist in denying that they have any disagreements and get mad at me for being so pushy about conflicts. In such cases, I work with the individuals on their fears and their childhood experiences with conflict, while keeping the affect level fairly controlled. Severe and persistent conflict-avoidant behavior in either spouse, is a strong indicator of childhood physical or sexual abuse. Fighting with a spouse may precipitate spontaneous feelings of unresolved anger toward a parent; when the individual feels unable to deal with that anger and pain, all conflict must be suppressed.

When the couple reports success in tolerating conflict and continues to negotiate day-to-day problems, it's usually time to move to the next stage.

STAGE 5: RESOLUTION OF THE PAST

Hypotheses

Couples in recovery experience pain and regret about the years spent in the struggle around substance abuse.

The loss is like a death—nothing can bring back the wasted years and the spent tears. This sadness is manifested in a variety of ways. There may be bitterness, anger, and a degree of coldness that keeps the partners at a distance, even when they are unaware of these feelings and believe that they have forgiven each other. Most frequently, the feelings are displaced onto some other conflict in the relationship; for instance, they fight about money or sex rather than drinking. It is natural for them to avoid looking in the mirror and truly seeing that time has past, that they are not young anymore and will never have a chance to start over.

As they begin to acknowledge the pain of their adult life, the older and deeper layers of hurt, particularly wounds from growing up in their respective families of origin, may come to the surface. Therefore, it is important to anticipate that opening up these grief issues may be overwhelming and precipitate a regression.

Finally, I assume that, in addition to the pain and bitterness about the past, there is an underlying issue about the couple's future. Once the partners can no longer scapegoat the substance abuse and their reactivity to one another has been reduced, the unspoken question becomes, "After all the damage we have done to each other, do we want to stay married?" Helping them deal with the past and address their shared pain is often effective in fostering the belief that despite the past, they have a worthwhile future together.

Goals

First the spouses must unite around the shared pain and sense of loss rather than continue their adversarial blaming positions. Second, they need to separate the past from the present, to attain some degree of distance and perspective, so that the story of the substance abuse years and the damage that was done has a beginning, middle, and end. Their future does not necessarily have to be determined by the past. Finally, I want the couple to appreciate that there is no cure for the past. Deep wounds leave scars and scars are often ugly; yet some people wear their scars with dignity and acceptance.

Strategies

Teaching acceptance. I ask clients how they think people come to terms with their destructive histories. Usually they assume that people forgive each other and put the past behind them. They explain to me the disease concept of alcoholism and the importance of not holding onto blaming others. While acknowledging that they are right, I take the opposite tack and frame some of the worst aspects of their past history as being *unforgivable*. This is particularly important in cases of physical abuse, sexual abuse, extramarital affairs, or refusal to participate in sex. In these situations the individual may be *unable* to forgive the spouse. I explain to them that it is possible for a relationship to survive and grow without complete forgiveness. Faking forgiveness is worse than accepting the notion that some things we have done to each other will hurt forever—just like the loss of a loved one. Trying to wipe the slate clean leads to denial. Acceptance leads to healing.

Rituals. All cultures have rituals for dealing with death, rituals that provide a way to respond to our helplessness, frustration, and loss. Death is death. The past is over. The ritual is something to do in the face of there being nothing to do.

When couples have difficulty dealing directly with the sadness and hold onto anger and blaming, I encourage them to give formal expression to the pent-up anger and label it as their way of expressing sadness. Sometimes encouraging the blaming releases the grief. In this blaming ritual I ask both individuals to make lists of all the specific episodes in the marriage about which they still feel hurt and resentment. I encourage them to freely project blame onto their partners while making their lists, rather than applying their new learnings about mutual responsibility. I tell them to indulge once and for all in blaming and finger pointing, without restraint or regard for the other's feelings. The attack is to be seen as a form of grieving.

The spouses bring their lists to the office and take turns reading their litany of hurts. I remember my trepidation when an extremely angry woman brought a huge notebook. The first page was devoted to a recital of resentments about their wedding night 28 years earlier. She took a long time to read through her list. She started cold and distant; by the end she was crying and her husband was holding her.

When spouses are already able to acknowledge their sadness, I suggest a mourning ritual. I might ask them to bring in their wedding pictures and talk about the innocence, dreams, and confusion of the young man and young woman who smile brightly and blindly into the future. I ask them to sift through family pictures and talk about what they were like back then. In the case of Bob and Sally (Chapter 1), I asked them to bring in the family photograph album and discuss with me what their lives were like at different stages of the children's growing-up. Rereading old love letters, visiting a special place from long ago, or simply playing a particular song might serve the same purpose.

It is essential for the spouses to find their own meaningful rituals and way of expressing feelings. I usually provide examples of how other couples have gone through this stage and then ask them to pick a ritual that is right for them.

Supporting denial. Many couples cannot face the pain of the past as directly as described above. When couples are either in denial or openly afraid of bringing up the past, I encourage them to consciously decide not to go back into the past at this particular time. I do not label this as resistance. Many people in our culture successfully avoid dealing with grief; in this respect my clients are not exceptional. I gently label their avoidance as a way of dealing with grief.

I remember saying to one couple, "You don't have to do this stage if you don't want to. Some people need to open up the old wound and some people don't. You two are doing a good job of looking forward and working together. I think you both know how badly hurt you've been and I think there is a real strong, healthy impulse to protect yourselves from all the old feelings that might get stirred up in going back over the past. Let's let the sleeping dogs lie for now. You may need to open those issues up later in the therapy, or you may open them up on your fiftieth wedding anniversary, or you may never address them at all. I think you'll decide in your own way what's best for you."

Anticipating the return to distance. Dealing with the grief in this way often leads the couple to experience a powerful moment of intimacy. I prepare them as carefully as possible for the strong likelihood that such intimacy may be somewhat overwhelming and that they will probably retreat to more distant positions shortly after connecting around the pain. They should not be too surprised or hurt by the return of resentment and distrust. Intense intimacy is always followed by a return to normal distance.

I also remind the couple that grieving is a process like recovery— it lasts forever. I encourage many couples to adopt a once a year ritual of going back over the past, much as people reexperience grief on the anniversary of a death.

Outcome

These strategies are designed to help the couple mutually let go of their shared history. When they work well, the spouses move toward one another. Sometimes one or both find themselves immobilized by seemingly intolerable feelings of futility. I remind them (and myself as well!) that feelings of despair may be acute but do not last forever. If someone is too overwhelmed, I encourage him/

her to retreat from the intensity of the grief by distracting themselves or increase their frequency of meetings. If there is a relapse, it can be seen as a signal that one or both spouses cannot handle the pain and need to pull back for the time being.

STAGE 6: INTIMACY

Hypotheses

Just as substance abuse is invariably linked to how marital partners manage conflict, it is also intertwined with how they become intimate and sexual. Some couples have used the substance abuse issue to avoid intimacy and sexuality. Others may need chemical use in order to become close and sexual. Still others develop a pattern of becoming intimate during the reconciliation period after a major outbreak of drinking or drug abuse.

I assume that the substance abuse pattern has covered over each individual's internal conflicts around intimacy stemming from unresolved family-of-origin issues. Since a high percentage of alcoholic couple systems includes at least one adult child of an alcoholic, the process of seeking intimacy in a new way often involves letting go of old, familiar, and safe roles. Thus the spouses are learning how to become close not simply without the substance abuse but also without any positive role models or prior experience with intimacy.

Spouses who have completed the first five stages have already become more intimate. Throughout the process they have been learning to cooperate, tolerate conflict, and accept the past. Reaching the intimacy stage is like clearing an area for planting. The trees have to be cut down, the stumps pulled, and the boulders removed. Then the ground is thoroughly tilled and fertilized. By the time the couple arrives at the intimacy stage, some of the hardest work has already been done.

Goals

All couples have private and idiosyncratic ways of being intimate and sexual; these must be respected. My first goal is to help my clients discover a new balance of closeness and distance now that the substance abuse has been removed. Throughout the process I have been restraining them from working directly on this issue; now it is time to encourage them to focus on intimacy needs. I help them to separate reasonable expectations for intimacy from attempts to make up for unresolved family-of-origin needs. Coming to terms with their old grief in relationship to their original families is often a prerequisite to setting realistic expectations for their couple relationship.

Finally, it is critical for me to take a less central and directive role in this stage of the treatment. I have been very central and directive up to this point; obviously, spouses can become quite dependent on the therapy and on me. During this last stage of treatment I need to empower them to take more leadership in the therapy and to become more self-reliant.

Strategies

Family-of origin coaching. As I begin directly to explore spouses' images around intimacy and sexuality, I encourage them to address their unresolved family-of-origin issues, particularly as they are related to trust, emotional/physical/sexual abuse, and fear of intimacy. Having already addressed the pain of their own relationship, spouses are usually prepared to open up and deal with the old wounds from childhood. It becomes apparent how each partner may have played out a family-of-origin role and perhaps expected the marriage to make up for the past.

It is desirable to work on these old issues before focusing on couple intimacy and sexual difficulties, because the process of sharing one's own childhood pain and seeing one's partner's actually produces a considerable degree of intimacy in itself. As each individual opens up, I emphasize the spouse's vital role as listener and nurturer.

Frequently the family-of-origin work involves specific coaching about how to make peace with some members of the family, become more connected to others, or mourn the loss of someone. The other part of the work involves helping clients get in touch with their own vulnerabilities and find ways of taking better care of themselves. This also opens up the issue of how much they expected their marriage to make up for their childhood hurts.

Nurturance rituals. Before we pursue sexual issues I focus on enhancing the spouses' skills in providing and receiving nurturance. The partners practice negotiating their needs and taking turns being on the giving and receiving ends of attention. I suggest that each spouse give the other the gift of being catered to a couple hours per week. While the partners do this, they are to keep track of their feelings in the giving and receiving positions. Not surprisingly, both usually have more difficulty articulating their needs and tolerating their feelings when they are recipients. Being given to often brings up feelings of yearning and loss that can be traced all the way back to early childhood.

Building safety into sexuality. Since many couples have experienced an impaired sex life prior to, during, and after the active addiction phase, and since most have difficulty addressing this issue directly, creating a safe environment in which to deal with sexuality is essential.

If, as I explore the couple's sexual history and patterns, it becomes clear that there is significant impairment of either performance or frequency, it makes sense to restrain the couple from being sexually active. The spouses need to feel safe to express their fears and vulnerabilities without an intensification of performance anxiety. This is particularly important with men and women in early recovery, since they may be either physiologically or psychologically incapable of being sexual. Substance abuse may have been a necessary component of one or both members' ability to perform; without it they may be lost. This may manifest itself as specific sexual disorders, such as premature ejaculation and impotence, or more diffusely as inhibition of sexual desire or performance anxiety.

When I restrain the couple from sex, I may be greeted with the grim riposte, "I'm afraid you don't have to worry about that!" Nevertheless, deciding not to have sex takes off the pressure; it is easier than having the issue constantly open to question and wondering how and when they may begin to feel sexual again. Agreeing not to be sexual usually facilitates greater closeness, since much of their distancing behavior has been related to subtly avoiding any situations that may lead to sex. Thus, spouses develop rituals of going to bed at different times, having conflicts in the bedroom, allowing children to be intrusive, avoiding physical contact, etc., to protect themselves from their sexual needs, anxieties, resentments, and fears of failure. Agreeing not to have sex allows them to experiment with closeness and intimacy more safely.

If there is a significant sexual dysfunction, a thorough physical checkup is indicated before initiating sexual therapy. This is also the time to establish with the couple that, regardless of who bears the symptom, the sexual issue should be perceived as a mutual problem, with each person accepting equal responsibility for change. Finally, it is important to establish that both individuals are highly motivated to work explicitly on the sexual relationship. When sex therapy goes badly, the failure can almost always be traced back to one partner's initial reluctance or covert blaming of the other for the problem.

The choice of techniques depends on understanding the couple's natural style, the partners' private images about intimacy, and their own theories about how their sexual relationship may be improved. I carefully tailor my interventions to fit the couple. Sensate focus massage with exotic oils may seem pornographic to a couple who has always made love in the dark.

In order to become more comfortable sexually, most people need to feel safe, accepted, in control, and close. Also, there needs to be a way to make "working" on the sexual relationship more fun and less "work." Some of my ways of "working" with couples to develop these feelings are:

(1) When a couple is uncomfortable in making the transition from the business of life to a romantic mood, I ask each individual to practice showing romantic interest and making seductive overtures. The partner is instructed to come up with a loving, gentle, and lighthearted rejection. Knowing in advance that the turndown is coming allows the individual to risk being "sexy" without seeing the partner's response as a judgment. When the partner finds loving ways to turn down a sexual overture, defensiveness lessens on both sides.

(2) Another way of helping couples who have difficulty making the transition from everyday concerns to sexual relating involves encouraging them to schedule sex in a very straightforward way. This gives both responsibility of clearing their minds and getting

ready for love-making. Neither has to be responsible for putting the other "in the mood."

(3) Most couples struggle with trying to make their sexual experience completely mutual. I encourage couples to practice taking turns receiving and giving pleasure. It is surprising how few couples allow themselves the luxury of worrying about only one person's sexual pleasure at a time. Spouses usually have enormous difficulty giving and receiving feedback about their sexual performance; this taking-turns strategy encourages practice sessions in which partners talk about what they like and don't like in a comfortable manner.

(4) When anxiety is focused primarily on the mechanics of sex, e.g., premature ejaculation and orgasm problems, I will encourage partners to engage in foreplay that does not lead to either intercourse or orgasm. When couples have lost their sense of playfulness and excitment because of their performance anxieties and their routines, sometimes an intervention can be as simple as encouraging them to go "parking." Other couples will be more comfortable with the Masters and Johnson sensate focus approach that is more highly structured.

(5) When spouses' issues are related to tension and residual anger, leading them to avoid closeness or sex because it stirs up the old uncomfortable feelings, I help them to accept each other's feelings of hurt and anger in sexualized situations. For example, I might encourage partners to start "fooling around" and then to stop and openly share their uncomfortable feelings — feelings from which they try to dissociate. I suggest that they stop the foreplay and acknowledge their bad feelings, rather than force themselves to swallow these feelings in order to have sex.

Since this intervention is so difficult for most spouses, I give them a taste of it in my office by asking them to hold hands, maintain eye contact, and discuss angry or hurt feelings about their sex life. Sometimes it's a good idea for me to leave them alone for a few minutes.

I remember one woman who said to her husband, while holding his hand, "The way that you use me in bed makes me feel like I'm just a tissue to drop your stuff in. I feel like it doesn't matter if I'm there at all. It's like I'm just another one of your girlie magazines."

When it was her husband's turn, he said, "I don't feel like you ever really want to do it anyway. I feel like you just close your eyes and wait for it to be over. I've always felt like my wanting to do it was something bad that you had to put up with." They had spent years denying these feelings and becoming robots in bed. While sharing the feelings did not cure the problem, it did allow them the unusual experience of being sexual and true to themselves at the same time.

(6) Many people are so traumatized by their past hurts and resentments that it is hard for them to develop stimulating sexual images and feelings. Such individuals can regain the "spark" through the use of erotica, guided imagery, or sharing of sexual fantasies. I once asked a husband and wife to separately think about their sexiest encounter and then to put it into the third person and write it as a fantasy. They were to read the stories in the bedroom on a night of their choosing. Each wrote about an episode from their courtship and apparently the stories stimulated a replay.

(7) When individuals are uncomfortable talking about sex, I use metaphors and embedded suggestions. It really doesn't matter too much whether you're talking about who "comes" first or who loads the dishwasher right. I trust couples to translate my metaphors into the sexual arena. For example, I might say, "It's funny how some couples, once they've figured out how to divide up the cooking and the cleaning, end up getting more interested in gourmet meals."

(8) Separate individual sessions are useful for spouses who are shy and anxious about their sexual performance. In the privacy of the individual session, people can talk about some of their secret fears and desires and think about new behaviors without having immediately to translate these thoughts into an action. The session also provides an opportunity for them to discuss negative feelings about sex that they do not feel their partner can tolerate. For example, one woman candidly acknowledged that she was repulsed by her husband's body odor. She couldn't imagine saying anything to him directly about it, but she did intiate their showering together as part of foreplay.

Clearly, there are as many different strategies as there are couples. The most important element in working with couples is helping them regain or discover their own natural rhythm.

Outcome

It is essential that the therapist accept whatever form of intimacy feels right to the couple. It is hard to predict what pattern will permit a comfortable balance of closeness and distance for a particular pair. The therapist should not be overly invested in having clients find intimacy on his/her terms.

Frequently, couples move toward termination in this stage. I support their taking charge of their lives and moving away from too much dependency on the therapy. Because I have played a controlling and dominant role in the evolution of the couple's new relationship, termination can be difficult.

Several strategies lessen the trauma of ending therapy. First, I establish the principle that therapy is open-ended and that my role is analogous to that of a family doctor. They can always come back. Secondly, in the latter stages of our work together, I am less directive and make fewer suggestions. Finally, during this stage I am more inclined openly to share my limitations as a therapist, husband, and father as a step towards stepping down from the carefully constructed pedestal on which I have been standing throughout the case.

If the couple responds to the push toward intimacy with some form of regressive behavior, the therapist should interpret this as an indication that the work on the intimacy or the family-of-origin issues has been too intense. However, since this last stage of treatment is essentially a termination phase, a little regression is normal. I anticipate it with the spouses and I encourage them to handle the episode without my help, as a way of gaining confidence in themselves. I also need to be aware of my own possible overinvolvement and make sure I communicate that I don't need them to rely on me.

QUESTIONS AND ANSWERS

Any treatment model raises as many questions as it provides answers. Following are some of the questions I have been asked about the application of this model over the past eight years.

Question: How long does this treatment last?

Answer: This treatment will vary in duration. Potentially couples may end treatment at any one of the six stages. The model is designed not to force couples to go through the stages in lockstep order. On the contrary, couples are given the message that they can either withdraw from or recess therapy at any stage. For example, many couples need only the disengagement and differentiation stages to achieve a new stability in their relationship. These couples may use AA and Al-Anon as the stabilizing force in their relationship and maintain sobriety without an ongoing course of therapy.

The length of the therapy will be determined by the frequency of the sessions at any given stage. For example, during the differentiation stage, I want the spouses to be investing most of their energy in working with AA and Al-Anon and I do not want the therapy to create too much pressure for change; therefore, I may meet with the couple only once every two or three weeks. During the stages involving conflict management or resolution of the past, intensity of the work may require weekly meetings.

Another length-determining factor is whether the couple goes directly through the stages or goes through a process of making two steps forward and one step back in response to the therapy. Most couples do not go through the treatment smoothly; rather, they get stuck at various points along the way or find it useful to go back to an earlier stage in order to restabilize after some kind of regression. Obviously, each case is different; however, in general couples take about six months to a year to go through the first five stages. If they decide to do the last stage around family of origin and intimacy, that may take an additional six months to a year.

Question: What is different about the treatment model if the substance abuser is the woman and the co-dependent is the man?
Answer: I feel strongly that there are significant differences in the couple dynamics when the woman is the abuser. Women often become co-dependents and enablers because they are socialized to the role and are economically dependent. They feel that they genuinely do not have the choice of leaving. When the woman is the substance abuser, the spouse is much more likely to leave the relationship than to stick it out. The men who do stay in such relationships often reveal a strong underlying dependency on their wives,

which is covered over by her being the one with the "problem." The closest model to this complementary relationship is the agoraphobic couple system in which the helpless "little woman" is taken care of by the "big, strong" man. The inadequacy and dependency of the wife become part of maintaining the man's ego and masculine identity, i.e., "In the land of the blind, the one-eyed man is king."

This complementary couple system may also cover up significant chemical dependency on the part of the man, which is only slightly more under control than his wife's. It frequently turns out that the wife's drinking got out of control in part because she was trying to keep up with him, i.e., "if you can't beat them, join them." Given the complementary nature of the relationship, it is not surprising that the husband is often in greater denial than the wife and will frequently undermine her treatment. I have treated several families in which the only member of the family to acknowledge the severity of the mother's drinking problem was the mother herself. The husband and the children tended to minimize the drinking or deny it entirely.

Another fundamental difference is that in a high proportion of families, if the husband is not emotionally dependent on his wife's symptom, then he is likely to leave the marriage than deal with the problem. Thus, many women struggling with substance abuse are also single parents. Women in these situations often do not have the luxury of putting their recovery first because there is no one else to assume parental responsibilities. This situation puts a unique pressure on the mother and the children, particularly children who are already in parentified roles.

In the course of the treatment, the therapist has to be very sensitive to the husband's need to maintain a helper identity, as opposed that of co-patient. The shift of the couple from the helper/helpee complementary system needs to take place much later in the course of treatment, simply because of the degree to which the man is dependent on the overfunctioning role.

In cases where the husband is not dependent on his wife's being symptomatic, one of the main difficulties for the wife/mother in early recovery is that there is usually a very powerful expectation on the part of the husband and the children that the wife/mother make up for the past by becoming a super woman. This is a pressure that she is likely to feel herself anyway but it is a burden that makes it hard for her to take the time necessary for putting herself first, attending meetings, etc. When treating these single parent families it is important to develop a support system for the mother so that she can work on her program, and it is often necessary to accept the children functioning in somewhat inappropriate parental roles.

Another difficult treatment issue is that many men will have difficulty using Al-Anon, because men are not socialized to reach out to others for help. Al-Anon, by and large, is still dominated by women, and many men are uncomfortable in a group of mostly women. I encourage husbands of substance abusers to find a predominantly men's Al-Anon group, but that is not easy.

In responding to this question, I've discussed some of the different implications in treating the substance abusing family system when the abuser is the wife/mother. However, it's beyond the scope of this book to begin discussing individual developmental and cultural issues that differentiate male and female substance abuse problems and treatment.

Question: When do you involve the children in the treatment?
Answer: It varies case by case. Generally the kids are brought in during the early stages on an as-needed basis. They also take part in education about the recovery process. Since I am restraining the couple from change and keeping Dad in a peripheral position, it is often helpful to give Dad the active role of being the expert on substance abuse and recovery. Thus, I put Dad in charge of educating the kids about the disease concept and the use of self-help programs as a means of beginning to empower him.

Children are also brought in during the negotiation stage if the couple is actively dealing with parenting issues. Their presence allows the parents to practice their new skills of working together.

Finally, stage 5, resolution of the past, is enhanced if the children are encouraged to take part in the process. If it seems appropriate, I invite the children to share in the sessions their own loss and pain in response to having grown up in an alcoholic system.

Question: How explicit are you about the organization and structure of this model when you are working with a couple?
Answer: That depends on my assessment of the couple's style and

manner of processing information. Many couples experience considerable relief if the whole treatment model is laid out like an
adult education course. Others are intimidated by the notion of an
apparently rigid treatment curriculum; it is more useful for them to
work through the stages one at a time without my explaining the
whole process. I want clients to feel the safety and sense of order
that comes from having a plan; at the same time, I do not want to
impose on them a course of treatment that feels overwhelming.

Question: Do you ever use this model in a couples group?
Answer: I personally have not done couples groups based on this
model; however, students of mine have organized couples group
around these six stages. The format allows the group to maintain a
sensible structure and progression which makes the group process
feel safer for both the therapists and the clients.

Question: How does this treatment model vary depending on the
socioeconomic, racial, or ethnic background of the participants in
treatment?
Answer: Any effective therapy has to meet people where they are in
terms of their background, their values, their world view, their
essential personhood. Each of us, as therapists, needs to recognize
the benefits of adjusting style, expectations, and therapeutic values
to meet the needs, explicit and implicit, of our clients. As a white,
upper-middle-class male from a privileged WASP background, I
am mindful of the extent to which my values, attitudes, and beliefs
are subjective and by definition prejudicial. When I am treating a
poverty-stricken, overstressed couple, I have to be extremely careful not to impose my values of what constitutes success. On the
other hand, I need to avoid the patronizing position of assuming
that poor or uneducated couples are less capable of benefiting
from therapy than those with more advantages. Too frequently our
expectations are colored by our prejudices.

Question: What kind of therapist can best implement this treatment model?
Answer: This model is not dependent on the therapist's being char-
ismatic. In fact, after devoting considerable time to imitating Sal
Minuchin and other family therapy heavyweights, I have come to

realize that trusting my own style of relating to people is much more likely to be effective than trying to be somebody I'm not. The therapist does need to be comfortable being assertive about the course of treatment. In addition, the therapist must recognize the dangers of overfunctioning, since the model itself puts him/her in a very central position. Often success is directly related to how adept the therapist is in moving out of center stage.

Do They All Live Happily Ever After?

Ruth and John came into treatment after he had been sober for a year. They wanted sex therapy. She hated sex and he desperately wanted it. It had been a source of tension and conflict since their honeymoon 28 years earlier—long before he had become an alcoholic. I restrained them from change because I thought opening up might threaten their whole relationship. I suggested that they spend another year working the program before dealing with sexuality.

A year later they came back and said they were ready for the sex therapy. Over the next six years they went through all six stages of my treatment model. We worked on their relationship, family-of-origin issues, coparenting, unresolved affect, and sex life. In the course of treatment, I met with their children and some of their siblings. I have given them the best therapy I have to offer. I care deeply for them and they clearly care for me. They have changed for the better in almost every aspect of their lives. Their sex life still doesn't work.

They have pieced together a livable compromise: She puts up with taking care of his sexual needs two weeks out of the month and he forgoes sex the other two weeks. He has let go of most of his obsession with sex. She has let go of most her resentment. And yet it still doesn't work for them. There is too much scar tissue.

I met with them the other day for a checkup appointment. They are doing well. John just celebrated his tenth anniversary of sobriety. There is a bittersweet feeling as we review our work together; our successes and our failures. The therapy doesn't have a fairytale ending. John and Ruth will not live happily ever after. And yet they have begun to make peace with what they can change and what they cannot change. They are learning how to live with their scars.

6

The Wolf in Sheep's Clothing: Child-focused Treatment When a Parent is an Abuser

Mrs. Carey sounded anxious over the phone. She spoke almost in a whisper as if she were afraid of being overheard.

MRS. CAREY   I would like you to see my daughter. Her school counselor says that she is in serious trouble at school and he thinks that she's using drugs.

D.T.   I would be happy to see all of you. Does she have brothers and sisters living at home?

MRS. CAREY   Her younger sister is at home. Her brother is away in college. He just started this fall.

D.T.   I would like to meet with everyone if possible. Is there a time when her brother is home from college?

MRS. CAREY   No, he's away except on holidays, and besides, I think my daughter would prefer to come in by herself.

D.T.   Well, I always start by seeing everyone in the family first. That way I get a chance to hear everyone's idea about your daughter's problem, as well as people's ideas about what might be most helpful.

MRS. CAREY   I'm not at all sure that my husband will come to a meeting.

D.T.   When would be a convenient time to schedule it for him?

MRS. CAREY   It's not so much his schedule, Dr. Treadway. Jack just doesn't really believe that counseling is helpful and he doesn't think that Lisa has a serious problem anyway.

D.T.   It would be very useful to me if he would come in, even if just one meeting, because I would really like to hear his point of view and get his ideas about Lisa's problems. Would it be best for you to talk with him about it or would you like me to talk with him this evening when he's home from work?

MRS. CAREY   I don't know what would be best, Dr. Treadway. He doesn't always get home until quite late and he may not want to talk. I guess I'd better talk with him when I get the chance. I'm not sure that Lisa will open up and talk with you if her father is there because they don't really get along that well.

D.T.   I would guess you're probably right. It may be more difficult for Lisa to open up with her Dad present. If she's upset about her Dad coming in, you can reassure her that it will be okay with me if she doesn't want to talk about everything. It's pretty normal for kids to be less open in front of their parents.

MRS. CAREY   Does my younger daughter have to come too? She's only 10 and isn't really very involved.

D.T.   It would be helpful to me if she could come. It might help her sidestep some of the trouble that Lisa has gotten herself into, and it might help Lisa feel less singled out if her sister has to come also.

   I hope that getting this meeting organized isn't going to be too difficult. It sounds like you might get an argument from just about everybody. Who do you think will give you the most trouble?

MRS. CAREY   Probably my husband. I don't think he's going to like this idea at all.

D.T.   I'll tell you what — explain to him that it will only have to be just this one time and that, in order to be most helpful to his daughter, I really need to hear his side of things, even if his point of view is that all therapists are full of baloney.

MRS. CAREY   Okay, I'll try, but I can't promise he'll be there.

D.T.   Give me a call if he's not going to come in, because I would like to talk with him over the phone about the meeting anyway. I really appreciate that this is hard, but I think I will be able to help your daughter much more effectively if I can get everyone's input right at the beginning.

This opening skirmish is hard work. Some therapists might call Mrs. Carey resistant; however, she is not the one who is being resistant. I am. It is completely normal for her to want to set up the therapy in a way she believes will work. I, on the other hand, want to set up the therapy to include all the members of the family living at home. This benign power struggle begins to frame the problem with an interactional perspective. In the space of a 10-minute phone call, Mrs. Carey has told me volumes about how her family system is organized. She and her husband disagree about how to handle their daughter. The husband and the daughter do not get along and Mrs. Carey seems caught in the middle. She seems protective of the daughter. I am already asking questions: Why is the Dad so peripheral? What's the relationship between the onset of the problem and the son's going off to college? Does Mom's reluctance to include Dad and the daugher's involvement with drugs indicate a possible alcohol problem with Dad?

Not uncommonly the alcoholic family's first contact with the mental health profession comes through a symptomatic child. Not all fathers who are difficult to engage in treatment have drinking problems; however, adolescent drug use and parental drinking of-ten go hand in hand. I always keep an eye out for the wolf in sheep's clothing.

When the child is presented as the "problem" and one of the parents is in trouble with alcohol, family members may be incapaci-tated and overwhelmed by the parental drinking and at the same time unwilling and unable to do anything about it. In some cases they may be terrified of the alcoholic's wrath: in others they may have accom-modated so thoroughly to the drinking and resulting behavior that they have become indifferent to and disengaged from the alcoholic; in still others the parents, having themselves grown up in alcoholic sys-tems don't really see the alcohol use as a problem.

The symptom bearer often represents an exquisitely mixed mes-sage to the therapist. On the one hand, the symptom can be seen as an attempt by the family to reach outside itself in order to get help; on the other hand, the symptom bearer diverts the family's atten-tion from the underlying substance abuse and related dysfunction-al patterns. The therapist needs to be prepared to work with both implicit messages.

Stumbling Blocks

The three most common problems with these families are:

(1) We assume the family is so dysfunctional that the child who is the symptom bearer needs to be rescued. Following this belief, we do individual treatment and help her understand that the problems in the family are not her fault and that she needs to have a life of her own. In many respects we end up in the role of a surrogate parent who competes for the child's affection and loyalty. The therapist tends to develop an alliance with the child against the family. The painful result is that the child is caught in a loyalty conflict between the kind, nurturing, temporary, imitation parent and the unsupportive, possibly abusive, but nevertheless permanent and familiar parents. Imagine the tension experienced by the child who has poured out her heart to her therapist about how awful she thinks her alcoholic mother is when her mother comes to pick her up at the end of the hour and asks her how her session went.

Ultimately blood is thicker than therapy. The kids will remain loyal to their families even when they are victims of abuse and neglect; thus, they will drop out of treatment or resist our therapeutic advice when they feel pressure to choose their own life and health over membership in the family.

This loyalty conflict was dramatically acted out by a 14-year-old girl who was being seen in individual treatment. She was the youngest member of the family in which all the other siblings, the parents, and all four grandparents were alcoholics. She was in therapy because she had a drinking problem. She developed a positive relationship to the therapist and for about three months stopped drinking, attended school, and stayed out of trouble. Everything seemed to be going so well that the therapist was completely taken by surprise when the girl attempted suicide the night before a scheduled session. She later reported later that she had felt as if she didn't have a family anymore, as if she didn't belong anywhere. Sometimes the choice between family and self is simply too much.

(2) We assume that the family wants help with the parental substance abuse. Thus, rather than trying to rescue the child from the family, we attempt to rescue the family from the abuse. This is

"the elephant in the living room" problem. To the therapist the drinking problem is so glaringly obvious and so instrumental in the child's difficulty that the temptation to address it right away is irresistible. So the therapist says to the family, in essence, "What about this elephant you have in the living room?" Often the therapist is quite surprised when the family says, "What elephant?" One must appreciate that confronting the drinking frequently means threatening the life of the family. The family has simply learned that it is safer not to see the elephant.

In one case I was treating a father whose drinking seemed to be elephantine, but no one in the family showed any concern. The elder daughter, who was the identified patient, was making considerable progress when unexpectedly the parents showed up for an interview by themselves. The father was quite obviously drunk. We assumed that this was a signal that we should address the drinking issue directly. During the interview the father acknowledged problems with alcohol and the mother freely spoke of how overwhelmed and upset she was. We thought we had done a brilliant job of timing our confrontation and thus were thoroughly unprepared for the family's dropping out of treatment. We heard nothing from the parents or children for three months; then they came back into treatment. Why? Because the daughter was symptomatic again. Of course.

(3) We attempt to treat the presenting problem without addressing the parental drinking at all. The classic structural family therapy intervention of empowering parents to take charge may be an excellent first step in these cases; however, the therapist has to be prepared for the backlash when family members recoil from empowerment of the alcoholic. If the therapist is not ready to acknowledge the family members' difficulties with the drinker and continues to endorse his parental authority, then they will frequently drop out of treatment or stop taking the therapist seriously. Even the drinker himself tends to feel ill at ease and inappropriate when in the position of parental role model and will tend to sabotage the therapist's efforts to empower him. In learning how to deal with this phenomenon of the whole family's resistance to the empowerment of the alcoholic, we have developed a specific treatment plan for this situation.

Harry and Mabel had three small daughters, the eldest of whom was having learning difficulties in the first grade. Harry was a chronic alcoholic who had been in treatment on several occasions. Mabel was a classic ACOA who had taken care of her eight younger brothers and sisters and effectively protected them from their abusive father and their apparently deranged mother. She had grown up poor in the hills of West Virginia and was very used to taking care of things. The only person Mabel couldn't seem to manage was Harry, but she was working hard on it.

When they came in for the first session, Mabel had all three girls decked out in their Sunday best with identical outfits. She was also dressed up and had on what looked like an Easter bonnet. Next to them Harry looked rather sloppy and unkempt. Since Nancy, the eldest daughter, was the presenting problem, I started by encouraging the parents to work together on how best to help her. It rapidly became apparent that Mabel wanted nothing to do with working with Harry; she basically considered him as one of her less competent children. Harry was also very skilled at displaying incompetence. As a beginning family therapist, I was sure that Harry needed to be empowered and Mabel needed to back off a bit.

The first week I put Harry in charge of communicating with Nancy's school. I told Mabel to take a little vacation from working so hard with Nancy and to let Harry help her out more. Harry cheerfully agreed to the task. Mabel listened to me very politely. In the next session she reported that Harry had been out drinking every night and had forgotten the assignment. Harry looked chagrined. Undaunted, I assigned Harry the task of going over homework with Nancy each night. Harry agreed and Mabel listened politely. The next week she reported that Harry had been unavailable to work with Nancy because he had had a car accident and was preoccupied with trying to get the car fixed.

Perhaps I was goaded by Mabel's obvious satisfaction in reporting Harry's malfeasance or maybe I just didn't know what else to do — in any case, I persisted in my effort to empower Harry. At the end of the session, I told Harry that I wanted him to plan an outing for the family. I encouraged Mabel to relax and enjoy the fact that Harry was taking care of the arrangements. Harry said that would be a fine idea. Mabel listened politely. The next week Mabel came in without Harry. She was clearly upset. She said, with a forced smile, "Well, we all had that outing you wanted us to have. I got to put my girls in the car and go visit my husband in the hospital because he got drunk, threw a fit, and stabbed himself in the stomach with a knife. It was some outing."

I finally got the point.

During my early years working with alcoholic family systems in which the child was the symptom bearer, I had ample opportunities to get into trouble in all three of these problem areas. I began as a therapist working with adolescents and tried to rescue kids from their alcoholic families. After I became trained in working with addictions and began to work with families, I confronted alcoholics immediately. During my family therapy training years, I attempted to stay focused on the child as the presenting problem while avoiding direct attention on parental issues, including alcholism. With each approach I had some successes. However, failure is a better teacher. Experiences like the one with Harry and Mabel have stayed with me. From them I have developed the five-stage treatment plan described below.

A FIVE-STAGE TREATMENT MODEL WHEN A CHILD IS THE SYMPTOM BEARER

(1) Engage the Whole Family

As was shown by the phone call with Mrs. Carey, trying to involve the whole family is not easy. However, it is through this negotiation with the concerned family member about who will participate in treatment that one develops tentative hypotheses about the family, e.g., who is in charge, who is central or peripheral, what some of the connections are between the problem and how the family is working, what family attitudes are toward treatment. Simply by asking for the whole family to come in I am frequently able to infer potential parental substance abuse because of the way the concerned spouse protects the other. The other main benefit of engaging the whole family is that it allows the therapist to define problems as interactional, i.e., between members of the system. This dramatically increases the options for change in both the family's perception and its behavior.

The main challenge in this first stage of treatment is to set up the therapy with the whole family without pushing the family member by making the initial phone call too hard and thus losing the case before it has even begun. The therapist needs to make an initial alliance with the concerned family member, who is usually the leader of the family. While suggesting that all family members come in, I also support the caller's ideas about the presenting problem, appreciate the difficulty of mobilizing the whole family, solicit advice about how best to approach potentially recalcitrant members, and encourage the caller to take a leadership role. Joining the concerned family member is critical at this juncture, since it is more than likely that the therapy will not happen or continue without his or her active support. It is also true that, since the therapy is likely to unbalance the status quo in the family, an initial alliance with the family leader is essential. In many respects the treatment will threaten their position in the family.

In Mrs. Carey's case, if she had continued to resist bringing in the whole family, I would have compromised. I would have let her win on the issue of bringing in the younger daughter while continuing to push for the husband's attendance. I would suggest very convenient times and offer to call the husband myself. I would even agree that I would "have" to see the whole family only for the first interview. If this did not suffice, I would acquiesce to her choice about who should attend, while stating clearly that I would need to see other family members at some point. I do not believe in telling prospective clients that they cannot play except by my rules. However, when I do agree to see a segment of a family, I usually make a deal that, as long as the symptom is clearly getting better and the situation is improving, then I will accept their decision about who belongs in the therapy. If the situation does not improve, then I will push them to call in other family members.

The problem of engaging the whole family is not resolved in the first phone call. Often the dysfunctional parent will not come in for the first meeting. I have found it useful to call the missing parent during the meeting, in front of the other family members, introduce myself, express my regret that he couldn't make it, ask if there are any issues that he wants to be sure are covered, and finally, set up the next meeting at a time convenient for him. I once had one of my students call a father while she was in the middle of a session with his wife and eight children. She cheerfully interviewed him about his fatherly concern for his children while the whole group sat and watched. It would have been very hard for the man to avoid either agreeing to come to the next interview or establishing himself as part of the family's problem by refusing to come in. If I cannot reach the missing parent over the phone, I might send him either an audiotape or a written summary of the meeting.

Since it is normal in alcoholic family systems for the mother and children to cover up for the father and generally avoid acknowledging that there are any problems in the family other than the one with the symptomatic child, I approach this issue of including the father quite carefully, so that the family members do not feel that I am attacking either them or the missing parent. I use a benign approach that simply presumes that fathers care about their children as much as mothers and have an equal desire to help their children. This rather calculatedly naive assumption tends to undermine the family's denial and to result in someone's deciding to educate me about the dysfunctional parent. For example, when I start to talk about phoning Dad in front of his wife and children, the kids may start fidgeting in their chairs, eyeballing each other, whispering, and even giggling. I can then casually ask about Dad and about their feelings about his attending the meetings. With Dad's role open for discussion, the family members have to choose whether or not to cover for him. Usually this results in an immediate rise in tension and confusion; regardless of their responses, it is quite obvious when they are trying to protect Dad.

Missing parents must be involved even if they have divorced, relocated, or died. Although I do not recreate original families by seeing divorced parents with their kids, I do make an effort to have contact with the missing parent. I treated one case where the two teenaged sons were being unmercifully disobedient to their mother. When I asked them about their father they fell silent and refused to talk. Their mother explained that their father was an alcoholic and had left the family, remarried, and moved to California. Since he had moved, he had not had any contact with the boys and had not responded to any of their letters or attempts to reach him by phone. When I announced that I thought it would be a good idea for me to call the father and talk to him about his sons, the sons thought I was completely nuts. I assume that the father did too, when I reached him by phone and said, "Hi there, I'm Dr. Treadway and I am working with your ex-wife and your two kids. Even though you have been out on the coast for a while, I would still be interested in your thoughts about the boys. If you don't mind, I would like to ask you a few questions." Naturally the man was surprised; however, he seemed willing to help. When I asked him why he had not had any contact with his sons, he carefully explained that since he had moved, remarried, and had two new children, he thought it was best for his boys if they just forgot all about him. At the end of the conversation, I thanked him for his time and asked him to write the boys a letter and explain his current ideas about his relationship to them, so that they could better come to grips with not hearing from him. He readily agreed to do that and thanked me for working with his sons. Naturally, this phone call did not lead to a letter from the father to the sons, but it did release the sons' huge backlog of pent-up anger, frustration, and hurt toward this father of theirs. On some level it was easier for them to face their father's irresponsibility and insensitivity after he had broken his promise to me. They seemed to take his rejection less personally and to see it more as a function of his problems than as a reflection upon them. The boys moved from blaming their mother for divorcing their father to appropriate anger at their father, then to understanding his alcoholism, and finally to their sadness and sense of loss.

Clearly the outcome of this first step is either to accomplish the job of engaging the family or to bring out into the open the issue of the dysfunctional parent. When the alcoholism is acknowledged, then family members have to choose whether to address directly both the drinking and the relationship between the child's problem and the parent's problem. Thus, regardless of whether Mr. Carey comes in for treatment, Lisa's problems can be understood and treated from a much broader perspective.

(2) Empower the Dysfunctional Parent

In most instances, if the problems with parental substance abuse are in the early or middle stages, then the first step of engaging the family does not lead to acknowledgment of any problems other than the concerns about the symptom bearer. The second step is simply an extension of the first. This involves continuing to relate to the family as though the dysfunctional parent is as involved and important as the overfunctioning parent. Thus, in the early session, when I asked Mr. and Mrs. Carey to discuss their concerns about Lisa, I gave equal weight to their answers.

D.T.   Would you tell your wife why you think Lisa really just needs to be left alone to grow up a little?

MR. CAREY   She knows exactly what I think. I've told her over and over again that she worries about the kid too much. It doesn't do any good to sit around and talk about this stuff.

D.T.   Well, what do you think should happen when Lisa comes in the house and she seems to be high on something?

MR. CAREY   If you ask me, I think she should be told not to do it and that there should be no big fuss about it. All kids these days fool around with drugs. It's completely normal.

As Mr. Carey and I are having this conversation, in which I am taking him seriously as a parent, the other family members are showing signs of acute discomfort. Mrs. Carey is staring straight ahead, with a somewhat glazed look in her eyes. Her hands work nervously in her lap, straightening and smoothing her skirt. Lisa sits hunched up on her chair, with her knees pulled up to her chin. She's looking down at the floor and periodically shaking her head in disagreement. Molly, the younger daughter, is fidgeting and restless. She keeps trying to make eye contact with her mother and her sister, but no one is looking at her.

After I have talked for quite a while with Mr. Carey, eliciting his views about his daughter's experimenting with drugs, it becomes obvious that Mrs. Carey simply cannot sit still and listen to this conversation any longer. She says, "I think Dr. Treadway, you should know that Jack sometimes comes home late from work when he's had a little too much to drink himself.

I don't mean to say that it happens all the time, but I don't
think he even notices when Lisa comes in high."

The tension level in the room jumps. Both of the daughters
sit up and look at their parents, first the father, then the mother,
and then back to the father again. The father just stares at his
wife in angry disbelief. I can feel my own anxiety mount as I
think about how to help the family face this issue without
blowing the father out of the treatment. My job at this point is
to maintain an alliance with the husband while facilitating
open discussion of his drinking.

MR. CAREY   (to his wife) I don't know what you're talking
    about. You make it sound like I come home drunk every
    night.
D.T.   Mr. Carey, does your wife normally complain about your
    drinking or did she kind of catch you by surprise today by
    bringing this up?
MR. CAREY   She brings it up at home from time to time, but I
    never thought that she would come into a meeting like this
    and say that in front of the kids.
D.T.   Do you think that Lisa here tends to see your drinking
    as a kind of excuse to do what she wants to do with drugs?
    My kid will nail me with the argument, "Well, you do
    it too, Dad," whenever he can. Do you think that Lisa does
    that?
MR. CAREY   I doubt she's even noticed that sometimes I drink
    more than I should, unless her mother talks about it to her.
    (to his wife) Have you been talking to Lisa about this?
MRS. CAREY   (responding in an anxious whisper): We have all
    talked about it. Even Molly has asked me about it after she
    had a course on drugs and alcohol at school.
MR. CAREY   Well, I'll be damned. I didn't come down to this
    meeting to have everybody talk about me. What's this got to
    do with helping Lisa anyhow?
D.T.   (thinking that Mr. Carey has taken all the heat he can
    handle for the moment): You know, it sounds like Lisa,
    without saying anything at all in this meeting, has managed
    to get off the hot seat. Why don't we just take a moment
    more to find out where you stand on this issue about drink-
    ing. Then let's get back to Lisa and what brought you all
    here in the first place.

As the session continues, we talk about Mr. Carey's drinking. Mrs. Carey and Molly acknowledge that they think he has a problem while he says that there is no problem and that he has his drinking completely under control. Furthermore, he says, it is no big deal if sometimes he drinks a little too much — it is not the same as using pot or whatever other chemicals Lisa is using anyway. Lisa refuses to talk about it and yet her eyes fill with tears. Even though there is no agreement, the issue is out in the open.

The abrupt exposure of Mr. Carey's drinking as a family issue is not typical. In most cases the indicators of the parental drinking problem emerge more subtly over several sessions. When gathering information about family background, it is useful to casually insert questions about the family's pattern of alcohol use, beginning with the parents' concerns about the children's use of chemicals, reviewing how alcohol and drug use was dealt with in the parents' families of origin, and then moving to the parent's own pattern of drug and alcohol use. When the issue does not come out directly, as it did with the Carey's, this line of questioning elicits family concerns about drinking. In order to avoid arousing the alcoholic's defensiveness, the therapist should not challenge him directly; rather, the confrontation should come from the family. Invariably, if the therapist confronts the drinker prematurely, the family members will unite to protect the drinker. On the other hand, it is also important to recognize the distress experienced by the spouse and the children when the therapist treats the drinker as a competent parent and accepts his word about his drinking behavior. I use their obvious discomfort to broach discussion among the family members about drinking and their differing points of view about it. My job is to avoid taking sides while validating each person's perception of reality. I scrupulously avoid turning the parent into the identified patient until it is clear that the family is truly ready for that to happen. There are grave risks for the family, as well as for the drinker, in naming the alcohol as the main problem, since once that is done there is no going back. This confrontation clearly threatens the whole family.

In order to raise the subject of substance abuse without losing the case entirely, the therapist has to manage a delicate balancing act. At such moments, I imagine what it must feel like to be a tightrope walker who suddenly, in the middle of his act, looks down. He realizes that he cannot go back any more safely that he can go forward and that each compensatory effort he makes in one direction may precipitate a fall in the other.

In the Carey case, my main concerns were threefold. First, I was worried that Mr. Carey would respond to the session by feeling attacked and therefore drop out of treatment. Secondly, I was concerned that Mrs. Carey would feel that she had betrayed her husband and would, out of fear and anxiety, pull the family out of treatment. Conversely, she might feel that my supportive attitude toward her husband, in which I accepted him as a fully functional and responsible adult, was offensive, leading her to pull the family out of treatment. If I lost the husband, I might still be able to continue working with the family while focusing directly on the alcohol issue and its relationship to the presenting problem. However, if I lost Mrs. Carey, then I would undoubtedly have lost the case. Thirdly, I was worried that Lisa might have an acting-out crisis following the session and thus protect the whole family from having to address Dad's drinking. It is not uncommon for the scapegoat to provide a crisis good enough to enable the family to return to therapy without ever mentioning the previous concern about the Dad and his drinking problem.

My job at this difficult moment is to maintain my alliance with Mr. Carey while supporting Mrs. Carey in her awkward position of having brought her husband's drinking problem out into the open. I usually strive for a delicate balance by refocusing on the scapegoat, a maneuver quite familiar to the family. While this feels like deliberate exploitation of the scapegoated child, it is often the only way to keep the family engaged in treatment and thus eventually help the scapegoat escape from her role in the family.

After we had arrived at an impasse around the issue of Mr. Carey's drinking, I shifted to questions and concerns about Lisa and how she was doing at school and with her peers. Lisa barely spoke and yet everyone became perceptibly more relaxed and comfortable now that we were back on the familiar territory of how best to deal with Lisa. Even Lisa looked less tense than she did during the discussion of Dad's drinking.

At the end of the interview, the following conversation occurred.

D.T.   Mr. Carey, I think it might be very useful to check with other people at Lisa's school to see if they share the same concerns as Lisa's guidance counselor. Perhaps the counselor is being a bit of an alarmist. Between now and when I see you all again, could you give someone, such as her home-room teacher, a call and see what she has to say? And, in terms of this concern about your drinking, it's clear we're really not going to settle the question of whether you drink too much. I'm sure you didn't come down here today to talk about it anyway. (With this I keep the drinking issue open, but appreciate his feelings about it.) I'd just like you to give some more thought to what you think is an appropriate amount of drinking for you and how best to help Lisa understand the difference between adult use of alcohol and what's right for kids.

I am a little worried, however, that your wife is afraid that she may have made a big mistake by even mentioning the subject of your drinking and that there may be one helluva family argument in the car ride home. I hope that doesn't happen because I think Lisa needs both of you and that you are going to need to be able to work as a team to help her. (Here I join with his concerns as a parent.) Obviously, you really care a lot about Lisa and it makes sense that she should come first. Is that right?

MR. CAREY   That's right. I came to this meeting to help Lisa and I sure as hell didn't expect to have Lisa's problems blamed on me and my drinking.

MRS. CAREY   I never said that Lisa's problems were caused by . . .

D.T.   (interrupting in order to avert the conflict): Hold on, let's not start the fight now. Your husband may be angry at you for bringing up the drinking, but it is clear that you needed to mention it and I don't think you were blaming Jack for all of Lisa's problems. Clearly, it's been a real concern for you. (I support her position.) I do think it would be a mistake, however, to let Lisa off the hook by focusing too much on this disagreement between you and your husband. I think you are right to be worried about her. She didn't talk much today, but my guess is that she's really having a hard time right now. Even though she may hate coming to these meetings and having the family talk about her, I think she really does need your help. (I refocus on Lisa.) I would like you to write her a letter this week and just let her know in a straightforward, not angry way that the things she's doing cause you the greatest concern.

D.T.   (to Molly, attempting to block the backlash around her bringing up Dad's drinking): I hope you won't worry that Dad will be mad at you because you talked about his drinking today. I'm sure that he knows that you were embarrassed about being asked to talk about it. He's probably going to be a little mad at your mother about this whole thing, but it's certainly not your fault. Isn't that right, Mr. Carey?

Somewhat reluctantly, Mr. Carey nods in agreement.

D.T.   (to Lisa, making a link between the symptom and the drinking): What are the chances that between now and the next session you're going to get into a lot of trouble, so that this whole uncomfortable topic of whether Dad drinks too much gets forgotten about completely?

Lisa sat up in her chair and for the first time in the whole session looked at and spoke directly to me: "My getting in trouble has nothing to do with Dad or anyone else in this stupid family. That's dumb."

I agreed with her that it might be a "dumb" idea and said that we would see the following session how she had done. As I watched Mr. and Mrs. Carey, Lisa, and Molly file out of the room, I had no way of assessing whether the session should be termed a success or a failure. Mr. Carey looked grim and his wife looked as anxious as ever, although she managed to give me a genuine smile as I shook her hand. Lisa extended a "dead fish" handshake and did not look at me at all, while Molly gave me a warm, friendly smile and seemed much more relaxed and relieved as she left the room. Would they come back or drop out? Did I push too far into the drinking or not enough? Would Lisa act up and distract the family as predicted? I would not know the answer to these questions until the next interview.

The difficulties encountered in this interview are typical of the second stage of the treatment model. Empowering the dysfunctional drinker without losing the family is a delicate procedure; the therapist has to be prepared for a variety of outcomes. Most importantly, the therapist cannot be overly invested in a particular outcome. Regardless of what the family does, the therapist needs to appreciate the outcome as information about how the family works and what position the therapist needs to take in order to work effectively with its members.

If the mother drops out, then frequently a follow-up phone call will elicit her feeling that I had been too supportive of her husband and did not take the drinking seriously enough. At those times I am quite candid about my approach to adult drinking problems and attempt to develop an alliance with the wife around our mutual concern about the drinking. I assure her that I will definitely address the abuse and will help her husband confront it. If she drops out in order to protect her husband, then I invite her to return with the kids but without the husband if that would be more comfortable. I might even ask to speak directly to the husband and get his approval to meet with the wife and children alone. I continue to relate respectfully to the husband while beginning to shift toward the wife's view of the problem. These moves are predicted on the assumption that the wife is the overfunctioner in the family and will ultimately decide if therapy continues. Obviously, if the husband is the overfunctioner and the wife is the drinker, then these roles are reversed.

If the husband drops out, then I help the others deal with their sense of guilt and anxiety while beginning to raise more directly questions about the father's alcoholism, the family's response to it and ultimately, the family members' readiness to confront it. Usually, if they are interested in continuing without father, then they are ready to address the drinking head on.

Most commonly, the family will come back and still be organized around the child who was the presenting problem or, as I predicted in the Carey case, the child will have a severe enough crisis to refocus attention on her. In this case, I move with the family back to the presenting problem. If I persist in bringing up the drinking issue, it is likely that the family will coalesce in resisting me while protecting the drinker.

The following session, all the Carey family members arrived thoroughly united by Lisa, who has been suspended from school for the first time. I could not resist pointing out the accuracy of my prediction about her getting into trouble; they all agreed among themselves that the previous session had *nothing* to do with Lisa's problems. In fact, Mom and Dad were in remarkable agreement that Lisa's problems were really the result of her hanging around her friend Debbie, who was clearly a bad influence on her.

I used to regard this kind of an outcome as a defeat; now I recognize that in reality it is closer to a draw. The family members have retreated from dealing with the drinking issues in a protective manner, and yet at the same time they are willing to continue the therapy. I assume this means that they were not ready to push into the parental issues and need to remain organized around the scapegoat until they feel safer and better prepared to deal with the drinking. I have learned that, if I simply accept the family's choice and work directly with the child-focused problem, then I usually will have another opportunity to address the drinking later on, if that is still necessary. In some cases, a successful resolution of the presenting problem does lead to some significant shift in the parental behavior and a literal reduction in drinking. Generally, however, resolution of the child's problem will result in the family's feeling strong and safe enough to deal with the drinking directly.

(3) Shifting the Symptom Focus

The basic assumption of the second stage is that empowering the dysfunctional parent will tend to break down the family's enabling and denial and result in bringing the issue of parental substance abuse into the open. In the third stage our task is to make the transition in focus from treating the presenting problem to working with the parent's alcoholism directly.

The key risks in making this shift in focus are similar to those of the previous stage: The drinker may not be ready to address the alcohol abuse in a motivated manner; the family members may be unable or unwilling to confront the drinking; and the child may "rescue" the family by creating a distracting crisis.

The therapist needs to maintain the alliance with the alcoholic while setting up the shift in focus and ultimately a confrontation around the drinking. This effort to ally with the drinker puts the responsibility for confronting the drinking on other family members, further undercutting the natural propensity toward family protectiveness and denial. While I am supportive of Dad, they are free to be tough on him with less feeling of ganging up on him or being disloyal. By the time the actual confrontation around the drinking takes place, my efforts to develop a relationship with the alcoholic bear fruit, since voicing the diagnosis of alcoholism in the context of a positive relationship between drinker and therapist can be relatively benign and acceptable. The obvious danger in this approach is that the family members will misconstrue my continuing supportive relationship with the drinker as being opposed to them and "on his side." Clearly I am in an awkward position—on the surface I am relating supportively to the drinker while covertly I am aligning with the family members and their complaints about drinking. While each case demands its own idiosyncratic approach, in general I urge the drinker to be understanding of his wife's and children's anxieties about even bringing up the drinking issue and elicit his help in encouraging them to speak openly about their concerns.

The next step is to suggest that the drinker do some variation of a controlled drinking contract. This will give him a chance to demonstrate that he really does not have a drinking problem and that his drinking should not be the center of attention. This is quite similar to the initial stage of couples treatment (see Chapter 3). In making this move I am assuming that, if the individual really is in trouble with alcohol, he will not be able to keep to a controlled program for very long; thus, by even his own standards he will have to admit difficulty with managing alcohol. I often initiate the idea of a controlled drinking contract by suggesting that it will be very helpful for the child who is the presenting problem if the drinker can demonstrate such self-control. Thus, I shift the focus while maintaining the drinker in his role as parent.

After Lisa's suspension from school, the issue of Dad's drinking completely disappeared for several sessions, while the family focused on Lisa. Mom and Dad worked together on setting limits and Lisa actually became more open and direct as she struggled with both parents. I continued to be supportive of Dad in his role as parent and also of the parental coalition in relationship to

Lisa. Obviously, this meant being on the receiving end of some of Lisa's wrath; at one point she compared the experience of being in the therapy with going to the dentist and being tortured by the Spanish Inquisition—all in the same diatribe. As usual I felt uncomfortable about the unfairness of maintaining Lisa in her scapegoat position; yet, I was confident that we would get back to the parental conflicts when the opportunity arose and that dealing with those would, in turn, truly take Lisa off the hook.

In the fourth session Jack (Mr. Carey) complained to me that Elaine (Mrs. Carey) had made a big fuss over his drinking the night before in front of the kids. He felt that she was undermining his authority as a parent. Clearly, Jack expected me to support him and criticize Elaine. I felt that, since (1) the family had made considerable progress, (2) Lisa was doing generally better, and (3) I had a good working relationship with Jack, now was the time to open up the drinking issue again. I responded to Jack's complaint by taking a careful history of his drinking and his wife's concerns. Jack was routinely drinking four or five stiff drinks a night; yet he was very confident that he did not have a drinking problem because, as he said, "I've never missed a day's work in my life."

D.T.   Listen, Jack, I hate to tell you this, but alcohol is a much more vicious drug than any of us were brought up to believe. From what you're saying you may have more dependency on alcohol than you realize. It doesn't really matter that you have never missed a day's work. I also think that, whether she says it out loud or not, Lisa thinks she doesn't have to listen to you on the subject of her messing around with drugs and stuff because she sees you going for the liquor cabinet every night as soon as you get home.

I think it would be a good idea if you set a standard of alcohol use that you could really live within and stick to it. That would show Elaine and the kids that you really are in control of the drinking thing and that you won't let it get out of hand. You've agreed that scenes like staying out late drinking with the guys and not coming home until midnight are not great. I would like you to set some predictable guidlelines; then, if you can't stick to them, I would like you to be willing to acknowledge that maybe you really do have a drinking problem.

JACK Everybody overdoes it sometimes.

D.T. Right now, I'm not concerned about everybody, Jack. The other thing is that both your wife and Molly have said that they are really worried about you. Lisa hasn't said much but my guess is she's worried too. Molly even said that she talked to Robbie about it before he went off to college. Since he hasn't been to any of these meetings and probably is less influenced by other people's opinions because he's older, I think it would be a very good idea if you would call him up and ask him to tell you straight out whether or not he's ever been concerned about your drinking. Don't be surprised if he kind of hedges a little bit in his answers, because he'll be unsure about whether you really want him to tell you the truth. Do you think you can get him to be honest with you?

JACK I don't know. He's kind of the family diplomat.

LISA He won't say anything at all. Robbie knows about Dad, but he would never say anything about it, especially to him (gesturing toward her father) He would be too chicken.

JACK Don't talk about your brother like that.

D.T. I don't know, Lisa. It sounds a little like the pot calling the kettle black. You haven't exactly been open with your Dad about your feelings about his drinking, have you?

LISA I don't say anything about it because this is all a joke. He's never going to do anything about his drinking anyway. And she's not doing anything about it either and this whole family is full of it.

D.T. I disagree with you, Lisa. I think that your Dad does take the issue seriously. I believe that he will be willing to work out a drinking plan that will help him either show the family that he can handle alcohol just fine or discover that alcohol is really a problem and that he needs to cut back drastically or even quit drinking entirely. Frankly, I don't think your Dad would be coming to these meetings if he didn't want to see things improved for you and everyone else in the family. He knows that his drinking has worried everybody. Are you saying that your Dad wouldn't deal with his drinking if he found out that it was a problem? What do you think, Molly? Do you think your Dad would do something about his drinking if he found out that it was a problem?

MOLLY I think he would, but I don't know.

D.T.   I think your kids need to know from you, Jack, that, if it turns out that you can't keep to the plan, then you'll do something about your drinking.

JACK   I don't think I'll have any problem sticking to a plan. I think this whole issue is a complete red herring.

D.T.   That's fine — just as long as the kids and Elaine know that if the plan doesn't work then you will treat the drinking as a serious problem.

"Hoist by his own petard" is an expression meaning that someone is caught in his own trap or plan. This is the point of a controlled drinking contract. I am asking Jack to take responsibility for his drinking in front of his family, to establish his own standards for appropriate alcohol use and then live within them. In most cases, the inability to live within limits, no matter how liberal, forces the drinker to see his own addictive relationship to alcohol. It's clear that Jack is feeling the pressure, and yet he's not being confronted in a way that allows him easily to fight back. I am actually taking his side and disagreeing with Lisa.

Obviously, while I am supporting Jack in setting up this controlled drinking contract the others are experiencing a considerable mix of feelings. On the one hand, they are relieved that Dad is being protected; on the other, they are frustrated and discouraged by my seeming to support his ability to manage alcohol. I make it clear to them that I understand that Jack's drinking program may not be acceptable to them even if he does succeed in sticking to it. The controlled drinking contract is simply a way for Jack to define his own standards about his drinking. Elaine and the children then need to decide how much alcohol use they can tolerate. I also say to Elaine, in front of Jack, that if he cannot keep to the contract then I will assume that he is an alcoholic. In that case, because of the nature of the disease, Jack simply may not have voluntary control over his use of alcohol. I tell Elaine that, if he cannot keep the contract and will not seek help, then I will help them confront him in a concerned and loving manner, i.e., by doing a family intervention.

Naturally, this discussion offends Jack. Nevertheless, it is important to educate both Jack and the family members about the disease concept in the eventuality that Jack cannot stick to the contract. I also recommend to the Careys that, while they are waiting to see how Jack does with his drinking contract, it might be very useful for them to try Al-Anon and Al-Ateen. When Jack objects to this recommendation I again ask him to be supportive and understanding of his wife's and children's anxiety rather than seeing the idea of Al-Anon as an attack on him.

(4) Resolution

Shifting the symptom focus from the presenting problem to the parental drinking has a dramatic impact on the family. Once parental drinking is clearly defined as a problem and positions are taken within the family and by the therapist, then it is very hard for the family to return to the prior status quo. In the resolution stage the therapist helps the family members deal with the consequences of this shift.

There are several possible outcomes of the preceding stage. First, if the drinker does make a drinking contract and then refuses to keep it, the family members' willingness to look the other way will diminish, especially since they have listened to the drinker make commitments and to the therapist who actively defends him. Generally, even if the drinker drops out of treatment, family members feel motivated to confront the drinker after they have bent over backwards trying to let him manage his own use of alcohol.

Second, the symptom bearer, that is, the kid with the "problem," may rescue the family by redirecting the family's attention to her. I go out of my way to anticipate this behavior with the family and make explicit the function of the acting-out as a distraction. In the Carey family I talked with everyone about whether or not Lisa would act out, whether Dad really wanted to resolve the drinking question or would be relieved if Lisa took the heat off, and whether Mom was ready to deal with the drinking, particularly if Dad didn't stick to his contract. I even raised the question of whether Robbie or Molly might have a crisis if Lisa stayed out of trouble. At the end of this discussion, Lisa made it clear that she doubted that the drinking was really going to be dealt with, but said she would be "damned if I am going to be everybody's excuse."

The most difficult-to-manage outcome results when the family members feel that I have endorsed the alcoholic's drinking behavior and abandoned them. When I first began to walk this tightrope between the drinker and the family, I frequently erred in being too supportive of the drinker and assuming that the family would go along with the thrust of the therapy and intuit that I was setting up the confrontation around alcohol. Some families simply felt that I was taking sides against them.

The approach described here is most appropriate for families in which the drinker is still quite functional and in the early to middle stage of alcholism. In more severe cases, it is important to move quickly to the diagnosis of alcoholism and some variation of family intervention (see Chapter 4) to help the alcoholic seek treatment.

I am also extremely cautious about doing controlled drinking contracts where there is any risk whatsoever of physical or sexual abuse in the family. This approach to confronting drinking problems in families where a child is the presenting problem and one of the parents abuses alcohol does *not* extend to situations where the parental behavior is physically dangerous. In those cases the therapist's first responsibility is to help the spouse and the children get adequate protection. Throughout this process of engaging and empowering dysfunctional parents the therapist needs to be sensitive to the possiblity of abuse.

The most common outcome is that the drinker fails to live up to his own standards of appropriate drinking behavior and then has to acknowledge that he does have a problem with alcohol. Obviously, this does not mean that the alcohol abuse has been resolved. All that has been accomplished is that the drinker and the family have successfully defined the problem and shifted responsibility to the drinker.

At this stage Jack went through several false starts at managing the drinking. He was abstinent for a month and then switched from hard liquor to only beer, in order to demonstrate to the family and himself that he was really in control. While Jack's initial attempts at dealing with the alcohol problem were generally doomed to failure, I encouraged the family and Jack in their efforts while continuing to educate them about the disease concept and why halfway measures generally do not work. I supported Jack as he explored these blind alleys while encouraging the rest of the family to be patient.

It is always difficult to judge when the therapist becomes part of maintaining the status quo rather than an agent of change. As I was beginning to worry about my role in the Carey case, wondering whether I had become an "enabler" by continuing to see the family without issuing an ultimatum to Jack to stop his drinking or go into treatment, I received a note from Elaine telling me of her decision to leave. She enclosed a copy of the following letter, which she had given to Jack.

Dear Jack,

We all love you very much. We want you to get help. Dr. Treadway has mentioned that there are treatment centers available and we think that you should go. In the meantime we are going to stay over at my mother's until you make your decision. We are all behind you and ready to work with you after you get some help to stop drinking. We know we all need to change.

Love,

Elaine
Lisa
Molly

P.S. Robbie says that he'll
come home this weekend and
drive you up to the place. He
thought you might be too mad at
me to want me to drive you.

I was surprised by the note. Had I waited too long before I confronted Jack? If I had been the one to give Jack the push, would Elaine have rallied to his defense? Would Jack go into treatment or would the case blow up into divorce? How come I felt left out when Elaine had not called me to check out her decision to move?

I had made my moves and worked my strategies. I had done a careful and well-organized therapy and here I was, at the climax of the work, feeling left out. The risk of a therapeutic approach as directive and structured as the one I have been describing is that the therapist can begin to believe that he is in control of the therapy and therefore not only responsible for the final outcome, but literally in charge of determining it. The Carey case was yet another excellent reminder for me that my treatment model is simply a vehicle that allows people to get to a new destination. Ultimately, regardless of my own personal biases, it is not my job to determine where people should go. Perhaps Jack would go into treatment. Perhaps they would get divorced. My job is to be the catalyst, not the judge.

(5) Recovery

The last stage in the treatment model begins with the family's full commitment to recovery and the beginning of complete sobriety. As was described in Chapter 5, sobriety is a profoundly destabilizing phenomenon for everyone in the alcoholic family system.

Jack Carey did go into inpatient treatment following Elaine's taking a strong stance. As is often the case, there was a brief honeymoon period during which the family members grew very close and connected. This process was facilitated by the family week program at the treatment center, which enabled the family members to deepen their understanding of the disease concept of alcoholism and both Elaine and the children to recognize their role as co-dependents. Jack "got it" about his drinking and became quite appreciative of the family member's commitment to him and their willingness to hang in there.

When the family came back into treatment with me I explained the recovery stages that I generally follow with families: (1) differentiation, (2) negotiation, (3) conflict management, and (4) resolution of the past. I encouraged them to proceed very cautiously, avoiding any significant changes in family organization and relationships. Jack was urged to go to AA regularly and Elaine and the kids were urged to continue Al-Anon and Al-Ateen, respectively. I also made it clear that Jack should not significantly change either his parental role or his relationship with Elaine. This was not a popular suggestion with Jack, who was filled with recovery evangelism and wanted to transform his relationships with everyone overnight. However, it was clear that Elaine and particularly Lisa were relieved that they would not have to feel obligated to change their relationship with him immediately. The other major question that I raised with the family members was whether they would have a substitute crisis both to maintain the old pattern and to test the strength of all the new changes. I told them the story of how my children always push me to the limit when I have vowed not to lose my temper because that's how kids test parents, learn to trust, and begin to risk showing their own anger. I wondered with them which of the kids would most likely put all these new changes to the test by creating a crisis. Interestingly enough, both Lisa and Molly suggested that Robbie might be the one because he seemed least connected with all the changes in the family and perhaps the most in need of attention. On their own the whole family decided to visit Robbie's college for the weekend, so that he could get some special attention without needing to have a crisis.

I knew my job was almost done. Slowly, I evolved into the family mental health doctor. They did not go through all the proscribed recovery steps with me, but they have stayed close to the program and used it well. A year or so ago, Molly took a turn at pulling a "Lisa" and I met with them a few times. Elaine and Jack worried well together. Jack's been sober now for five years. Last spring I received an invitation to Lisa's wedding. She wrote me a note at the bottom of the card.

Dear Dr. Treadway,

I hope you'll come. I'm glad you turned out to be wrong about me.

Lisa

7

Hanging on for Dear Life: Family Treatment of Adolescent Substance Abuse

The mother in my office was distraught. Her 13-year-old son had run away three nights earlier, after she had confronted him about the marijuana that she had found in his room. In therapy I had been encouraging her to take a tougher stance with the boy. When she had grounded him for the upcoming weekend, he had just turned on his heels and walked out of the house. She had called all of his friends' mothers, but no one had seen him. She had driven around town for hours looking for him, but to no avail. Each morning she checked at the school to see if he had come in. They had not seen him. She called the police; they had not been able to find him either. She even called her ex-husband who lived out of state. He responded by blaming her for ruining his son. She felt helpless, scared, and alone. She kept coming back to the question of where the boy had found a place to sleep. At one point she said to me, "You know, sometimes when I have to wake him up in the morning, I just stand there and watch him sleep. His face looks so soft and young. I look at him and he's still my little boy."

Before I had children, I was pretty good in these situations. I would encourage the mother to hang in there, reassure her that the boy was probably all right, and tell her that it would be good for him to find out how tough it might be out on the streets. The answers came easily to me back then.

My son turns 11 this year. Sometimes, when he is angry, his face takes on a cold, hard look. He looks like a stranger to me. Sometimes he tells me that he can't stand our home and that he wants to be free and to live on his own. A cold fear stirs inside me. I can imagine driving the streets late at night, looking. I can imagine the round of phone calls and the sitting around. I can imagine the waiting. Sometimes I find myself watching my son while he is sleeping.

The answers don't come so easily anymore.

*   *   *   *   *

Working with adolescent substance abusers scares me. By the time these children are in serious trouble with chemicals, the family, the school, and the community have often lost a significant degree of control over them. Their own self-destructive impulses have taken over. It was right for the mother to confront her child about the pot, but the risk was real. The streets are not safe for a 13-year-old.

For me the hardest part of working with adolescents is that, when it comes to a confrontation over control, many kids are willing to die in order to win. Adolescents are able to intimidate adults because they will got to such extremes in order to resist being controlled. Kids always have the power to hurt themselves. When a four-year-old angrily declares that he hates his mother and is going to live at his friend's house, his mother will shake her head and make the child get dressed anyway. When a 16-year-old says that if he can't go out on Saturday night he's going to run away from home and live on the streets, his mother and his father are quite likely to be immobilized by fear. Parents frequently need to be more assertive with their children, but it is profoundly hard to do when their adolescent has shown a reckless disregard for their own safety.

Parents do not really have much power, and neither do therapists. Work with out-of-control adolescents can feel like driving a huge tractor trailer that has lost its brakes and is careening down the mountainside. You can't stop the truck. Somehow you have to either run into a snowbank or steer it all the way down to safety. It's really a matter of hanging on for dear life.

There are several key elements that make working with adolescent substance abuse especially difficult:

(1) Since abusing chemicals is a rite of passage for most adolescents in our culture, it is sometimes difficult to distinguish between the adolescents who are going through the normal developmental stage of learning how to handle chemicals through experimentation and the adolescents who are in serious trouble. Yet, it is clear that many adolescents have real problems with handling chemcials right from the start. This is particularly true for children who are growing up in dysfunctional families. For many of these teenagers, who have a considerable amount of chronic anxiety, low self-esteem, and residual anger, the discovery of drugs and alcohol may be overwhelmingly powerful. The chemical magically brings them relief from anxiety, an enhanced feeling of self-worth, and often much greater ease in their relationships with their peers. For these children, normal experimentation can lead quite quickly to a pattern of abuse and then addiction. Yet, it is hard to distinguish between the kids whose abuse of drugs and alcohol is simply a part of adolescent acting-out behavior and those who really are drug-dependent almost immediately.

(2) Adolescents are quite resistant to treatment and are rarely candid about their use of chemicals with either their families or therapist. Thus, serious substance abuse can go unrecognized while the family and the therapist attempt to deal with poor grades, a surly attitude, and breaking curfew. When the therapist does attempt to confront the possibility of substance abuse in the adolescent, it may lead to the adolescent's escalating his/her defiance into a real crisis, which may include running away from home, threats of suicide, or a refusal to obey any rules.

(3) Once teenagers do acknowledge their dependency and seek to change, there is often little support or understanding within their peer groups. This is particularly true for kids who are trying to be completely abstinent. Adolescents who may desperately need a support group in order to stay sober feel like outcasts when they reenter their school and home environment after treatment. Having built their social life around their use of chemicals, they

have difficulty relating to their peers straight. For adults, AA and Al-Anon groups are so widespread that almost everyone can find a group that feels comfortable. Unfortunately, there are simply fewer self-help groups for kids.

FAMILY PATTERNS

By the time parents and adolescents arrive in my office, the parents have usually lost control of the child. The parents may have been too permissive and allowed the child too much freedom, or they may have been excessively rigid and controlling. Most frequently, the parents are split between permissive and rigid positions and thus provide an inconsistent and incoherent point of view to the child. Whatever particular positions the parents have taken, they are usually helplessly flailing at their surly, unresponsive adolescent and blaming each other for the problem.

When adolescents have too much freedom, they feel internally unsafe and abandoned. Thus, the escalation of acting-out behavior can be seen as an attempt by the adolescent to engage the parents and to force them to exercise some control and authority. It is developmentally normal for adolescents to learn how to define their own identity through the process of struggle with their parents and other authority figures. When the responses of the adult world are excessively rigid, permissive, or inconsistent, adolescents tend to become more out of control, as they anxiously seek both their sense of independence and the feeling of protection that comes from external limits set by caring adults.

During this invariably difficult time for developing adolescents, the family itself is undergoing significant stress and transition as it enters the leaving-home stage of the family life cycle. The parents have to allow their children progressively more autonomy. In addition, the parents have to renegotiate their lives with each other as they make the transition from being primarily a parenting team to being a couple. They may experience considerable unacknowledged anxiety about the prospects of facing their relationship after the children leave home. On an individual level, the mother may be putting more effort into her career, while the father is simultaneously arriving at his own mid-life crisis and coming to terms with the limits of his career and questions about his own future. Finally, adolescents themselves have to resolve their struggle between needs to be separate and unresolved dependency. A crisis with an adolescent has the effect of distracting the family from all these normal developmental processes and in that respect may protect family members from the stress of facing these transitions.

I remember a very striking case in which three family members (a father, stepmother, and son) came for treatment. The presenting problem was the son's heroin addiction. The family was in a rigid pattern of conflict, with the father caught between the son and the stepmother. The most salient aspect of the case was that the father was 80, the stepmother was 75, and the son was 49. The family had simply never been able to go through the normal developmental process of having the child successfully leave home. The family was in a tableau like the couple on Keats' Grecian urn, always chasing and never changing. The symptom allowed the family to maintain the old status quo while going through time. Not surprisingly, treatment, which had also become part of the family's pattern, was unsuccessful. In a five-year follow-up study, we learned that the father had died and the son had given up heroin. The urn had finally broken.

There is invariably tension between the adults attempting to manage an out-of-control teenager. Some adults will be sponsoring more support, understanding, and freedom for the child; others will be arguing that the child needs firmness, limits, and confrontation. The adults often actively undermine each other and this further empowers the child in the struggle. These splits between the adults appears in many different patterns. The husband and wife may be detouring their marital issues by focusing on the child. In a single-parent family the mother and the child may be reenacting the unresolved struggle between the divorced parents. In other families, the child may be a scapegoat who unites the family. Sometimes the split is between the family on one side and the school or courts on the other.

The common thread in each of these patterns is that there is significant disagreement among the adults about how to manage this adolescent. They split on the age-old debate between firmness/discipline and nurturance/understanding. Clearly, both elements are essential to growth. What frequently happens is that the adults involved become polarized, with each side pushing its position harder in an attempt to counterbalance the other. Thus, firmness becomes punitive and nurturance becomes enabling.

Six-Stage Treatment Model

Stage 1: Engage the Whole System

As in the Carey case described in Chapter 6, the first step is to engage the family in the therapy. I emphasize to parents that they are the ones who can most directly help their child in trouble and that my role is to facilitate their working with their adolescent more effectively. Almost always I have to counter the parents' response: "We've tried everything. You're the doctor. We want you to make him better." People often feel the need to remind me that I am "the expert." I usually accept that designation and use it to reinforce my efforts to get the family involved right from the beginning of treatment.

Engaging the whole system means doing considerable leg work to make contact and build working alliances with the other professionals working with the family. Since a very high proportion of adolescent substance abuse cases involves active splitting among the adults as to how to respond to the teenager, it is essential that I enter the case not on one side or the other but as someone who can help the various sides resolve their disagreements. For example, when a school refers an adolescent and the family does not feel that there is a problem, I establish my role with the school and the family as a potential negotiator. I don't represent the school's position to the family because that will usually stiffen the family's resistance to treatment. By the same token, I don't simply join the family by scapegoating the school. In order to establish my role as "honest broker," I show equal respect for both sides.

Careful networking to engage the other professionals can also be beneficial in providing leverage. Often the other professionals (school and counselor, probation officer, department of social services worker, etc.) have the clout to put external pressure on either the adolescent or the parents, if that becomes necessary. When other professionals are treated with respect as colleagues, they are often willing to collaborate on these cases and to play the role of the "heavy." This variation on the "good cop/bad cop" game allows me to be tough with the family without risking my alliance with them. In one case, the most critical interview in the whole course of treatment took place when the probation officer came to a therapy meeting and described in vivid detail what it would be like for the boy to be in a youth detention center. The family's level of cooperation rose dramatically after that session.

Stage 2: Assessment

The key question in assessing and treating adolescent substance abuse is: When do you treat the acting-out behavior as the main issue and when do you treat the chemical dependency as the central problem? This is particularly difficult when there is little clear-cut evidence of the degree of dependency. Here I use the same basic approach that I use in treating adults, which is to remain very vigilant to the possibility of chemical dependency while initially treating the presenting problems. The treatment itself becomes a diagnostic process. Adolescents who are using substances as part of the whole gamut of rebellious behavior will tend to be responsive to effective family therapy, but teenagers who are really "hooked" on drugs will generally be unable to respond to the family treatment. This failure to respond leads to the exposure of the drug problem in much the same way as the disengagement stage in couples treatment often leads to a confrontation of the hidden alcoholism (see Chapter 3). Using the treatment process itself as a diagnostic tool enables one to avoid the typical "cops and robbers" game, in which the parents make accusations about their kids' drug use that they cannot prove and thus set up endless rounds of recriminations and denial.

Rarely do families initially seek treatment because of an adolescent's problems with chemicals. More frequently the presenting problem is related to the child's performance at school or rebellious behavior at home. The parents are usually locked in a hopeless power struggle with the child, in which every position they take is quickly countered by escalating defiance. We first need to consider whether there is a substance abuse problem at all. Since kids generally do not volunteer this information in sessions, I am constantly on the alert for signs of a potential problem. The following are some habits and behaviors that strongly indicate potential substance abuse:

(1) Significant deterioration of school performance.
(2) Change of peer group and unwillingness to have friends meet parents.
(3) Significant swings in mood.
(4) Unwillingness to accept authority and limits, e.g., curfews and other responsibilities.
(5) Major disturbances in sleep patterns and eating patterns.
(6) Loss of interest and involvement in previously valued activities, such as athletics, hobbies, and church groups.
(7) An excess amount of unaccounted for money or possessions.
(8) An excessive need for money.
(9) Withdrawal from participation in family life.

Whenever I hear parents report a cluster of these behaviors, I consider substance abuse as a potential underlying catalyst for many of the adolescent's difficulties. Chemical dependency should also be kept in mind when assessing teenagers' resistance to therapy and difficulty changing their behavior. Adolescents are even less likely than adults to be able to manage their need for chemicals. The therapist should consider a teenager's inability to respond to therapy as an indicator that he/she is already too dependent on chemicals.

As in the case of hidden adult substance abuse, the adolescent's abuse is usually not out in the open. I begin by joining the family around immediate concerns. The primary task of the first session is to address the presenting problems. However, as part of the early joining I do ask circular questions about family members' feelings, philosophies, and behavior around substance use issues:

- Which member of the family worries about drugs the most?
- Which child is most likely to be drawn to chemicals and why?
- Which of your parents is most likely to understand why kids lie about their use of drugs?
- Which of your children would have the hardest time confiding in you if he or she were in trouble with chemicals?

- What are the most effective ways that parents deal with kids who abuse drugs? What are the least effective ways?
- What are the ways that kids learn how to manage their own experimentation with drugs and booze?
- (To the kids) What is the best way to help a friend who is in serious trouble with drugs and booze?
- (To the parents) How did your parents manage this issue? What was helpful and what was not helpful?

These questions are not simply thrown at the family; rather, they are worked into the general questions about how the family works asked at the beginning of the first couple interviews. The questions usually allow the subject of adolescent substance abuse to be brought up and discussed without threatening or accusing anyone. When the parents do begin to accuse the identified patient, I steer the conversation in another direction. How family members respond to these questions usually provides me with a strong sense of how much covert substance abuse is going on in the system, even though they have not been asked directly about their own patterns of use. The clue may be a giggle between siblings, a slight shake of the head, a description of a friend's problem, or an evasive answer. What is most important for me is not the exact amount of substance abuse but the fact of possible covert abuse and the family's repertoire of ideas about how to address it.

In addition to opening up the topic of drug and alcohol use in a general way, I normalize adolescents' experimentation with chemicals and their dishonesty with parents and therapists about such experimentation. Rather than getting caught in a game of "Miami Vice," in which the parents try to get the "goods" on the teenager, I encourage them to focus on observable behavior and whether or not the child is making any progress on that front. I review with the parents and the adolescents the behavioral indicators of substance abuse outlined earlier. Just as with a controlled drinking contract, I set up the therapy as a potential test of whether the adolescent is out of control with chemicals. I explain to the parents that genuine progress in the therapy may indicate that the child is managing his/her covert experimentation with chemicals responsibly and that a lack of progress or cooperation in the therapy may signify that there is a much bigger problem with substance abuse than anyone in the family suspects.

This benign double bind, which naturally infuriates adolescents, sends a strong message that, if they do not cooperate with their parents, their use of chemicals will come under much greater scrutiny. It also sets up in advance the possible shift from treating the child as simply an acting-out adolescent who needs limits to thinking of him as a drug-dependent child who is out of control and needs to be treated as "sick" rather than "bad." Frequently, when the limit-setting confrontational approach does not work, it is because the adolescent cannot control his need for chemicals and thus is unable to respond to the treatment.

Stage 3: Empower the Parents

Since parents usually enter therapy only when they have already lost effective control of their adolescent, our task is to empower them so that they can respond more effective to their teenager. The initial strategies involve having the parents stop flailing at the adolescent in a way that perpetuates their sense of helplessness and inadequacy. Empowering parents means helping them take charge of their own responses and become less reactive to the adolescent.

This process begins with the conduct of the interview and the therapist's way of responding to the struggle between the parents and the adolescent in the room. I invariably make an alliance with the parents around the difficulties of managing their children rather than maintaining a neutral and evenhanded position. Although I truly enjoy kids, including thoroughly obnoxious, mouthy adolescents, I do not undercut the parents by making an alliance with the children, particularly at the parents' expense. Invariably, this means that parents feel supported by me and kids feel that therapy is some form of punishment initially.

In one first interview with a mother and her adolescent son, the boy reviled the woman in extremely vulgar language. She sat motionless, like a frightened child being berated by an abusive parent. Being a very astute clinician, I sensed a possible problem in the hierarchy. When I encouraged the mother to confront the boy, he simply became louder and more abusive and turned some of his abuse toward me. I was in a dilemma. If I confronted him successfully, then I would have saved the mother, but I also would have disempowered her even further. If I didn't confront the boy, then I would essentially be taking the same helpless position that she was taking. Finally, I said to her, "It is really helpful to me that you are letting your son demonstrate how angry and rude he is. If you had insisted on his behaving better in our meeting today I never would have had such a clear sense of how difficult he must be to manage at home. Would you like to continue to let him berate you for the rest of the hour, or would you like to simply excuse him from the room if he can't keep from swearing at you?"

Reframing her behavior in this way did not create a dramatic shift in the hierarchy. It was only the beginning of her learning that she had a choice. She told the son to leave the room.

There are many ways for therapists to empower the parents in the room. It is useful to talk to parents first and encourage them not to allow interruptions by obstreperous children. The parents should decide whether it is better for them to talk with unresponsive teenagers or ignore them when they will not participate. I point out that it is not their responsibility to make the child talk in the session. I also prepare parents for the possibility that the teenager might bolt from the room if the session gets too difficult. I encourage them not to be overly concerned if this happens; it simply means that the adolescent was unable to communicate in any other way that he was feeling too much pressure. Since I began giving this message to parents, fewer adolescents have found it necessary to precipitously leave the room.

Despite this focus on allying with the parents, it is important to make the therapy a safe place for the kids also. I make sure that they have opportunities to present their points of view about how the family works and to voice their complaints about their parents. It often helps to put kids at ease by telling them that it is normal and appropriate for them to maintain a sense of privacy about themselves and that it is okay if they do not want to be totally open with their parents, siblings, and me. When an adolescent won't talk at all in the session, I tell parents that they should not attempt to force him to talk; rather, they should just accept that, although he may not be ready to express himself, he can't help listening.

The primary difficulty in empowering the parents is resolving the split between them about how to manage the children in the first place. Since the struggle over the adolescent is often a metaphor for other unresolved issues between the spouses, it may be difficult for them to formulate a united plan of action. Patiently helping the couple negotiate and struggle over how best to respond to the child is essential. It is important to keep the identified patient in the negotiating process, since the experience of watching the parents learn how to work together allows him/her to begin to give up the role of protective lightening rod.

I also keep the siblings involved because building some bridges among the siblings in the system allows me to broaden the problems from simply the difficulties of this "bad" child to less toxic general parenting issues with all the children. In one part of the room the parents may be involved in negotiating a new set of rules, while in another part the siblings are working on what they as a group would like to see changed in the family. The parents may take some time to work out a particular position vis-à-vis the child in trouble; then one of them will be selected to negotiate the new parental position with the child. When the parent gets into a snag with the kid, I encourage both parents to go back to their discussion and work on their response to the teenager's objection. Whether the parents are able to struggle through to a consensus or end up agreeing to disagree is less important than the process of their confronting each other directly and learning how to negotiate. I normalize disagreements and encourage the parents to accept the value of their having different perceptions and solutions. I help the parents practice taking turns being in charge, presenting a united front, and even working independently.

At this stage, however, I am careful to keep the focus of the negotiation on parenting rather than allowing them to open up marital conflicts. If the parents begin to expose their marital fights, the adolescent is likely to act out again in a distracting and protective manner. I almost always keep the kids in the room and engaged in the process, because then it is much easier to keep the parents focused on parenting.

When there is only one parent involved, I help the parent lay out her agenda for the session and then direct her to engage the child. When the parent gets caught in a struggle, I help her sort out the range of possible responses. I work only minimally with the kids. If I engage the kids too much, then I inevitably slip into the role of the missing parent; that often disempowers the single parent even further. As I mentioned in Chapter 6, I also engage the other parent in the treatment by contacting him and, whenever possible, having him come to sessions with the adolescents. This brings into focus the unresolved issues with the distant parent.

In terms of confronting the teenager's behavior, I direct the parents to work at setting limits only on the behaviors over which they have the possibility of exercising some control. For example, a rule that a child cannot smoke pot is impossible to enforce. However, a rule that says a child who gets caught smoking pot will not be allowed to use the family car is within the parents' power to enact. This is a particular problem when the child's attitude is a source of contention. It is virtually impossible to legislate a positive attitude, and yet parents will be drawn to confrontation over their teenager's surliness like moths to a flame. I tell parents that a negative attitude is worn by many kids like a fig leaf. It protects them from feeling too exposed. It protects their pride. The message to the parents is: "Focus on the behavior and don't get hooked on the attitude. There's no crime in your son's not feeling like doing what he has to do as long as he is doing it."

The key to effective empowerment is to have the parents set reasonable limits with practical consequences and avoid empty threats. The rules and consequences need to be adjusted to the age of the adolescent; also, at different ages the parents will have different forms of leverage. There are several elements that help parents develop effective limits and consequences:

(1) Involve adolescents in creating rules and consequences through the use of family meetings and contracts. Adolescents should be encouraged to make specific suggestions about how the parents might also work on their own behavior, so that the contracts are mutual rather than unilateral. Contracts that adolescents feel are fair are much easier to enforce than parental orders.

(2) Negotiate limits and consequences that are in line with the community standards for adolescents. It is very difficult for teenagers, who are so oriented toward peer relationships, to handle rules and punishments that are either significantly more permissive or significantly more restrictive than the

community norms. Whenever possible, work with other parents in the community to develop standards of behavior.

(3) Although it is useful for the parents to be flexible in creating the contract, once it is agreed upon they should be rigid in enforcing it. Contracts should be kept to the letter for an agreed-upon length of time; then they can be renegotiated. Adolescents usually want to change the contract the minute they get caught breaking one of its provisions.

(4) Choose consequences that can be applied without expressing a lot of critical or angry feelings. Parents frequently betray their sense of helplessness by resorting to angry outbursts. These tend to be harshly judgmental and much more punitive than a consequence administered without rancor.

(5) Apply limits consistently and do not be manipulated into modifying the terms of punishment. A relatively short-term punishment carried out to the letter is much more effective than a long-term punishment from which the parents ultimately retreat because they feel guilty about the harshness.

(6) Regularly adjust the contract and parental expectations to reflect adolescents' constant state of change and increased autonomy.

(7) With adolescents 17 and older, parents need to stop trying to control and direct the adolescent and to learn how to negotiate with the child as an adult. At this age, parents cannot legislate behavior; however, they can decide what they will and will not support. They cannot order a child to go to school, come in at a certain time, or abstain from drugs, but they can withhold financial support, forbid him from living at home, or insist that he pay room and board. The message to the child is that with adult freedom comes adult responsibility.

(8) Parents need to be reminded that it is normal and appropriate for kids to struggle with their parents. Adolescents develop their own identity and sense of autonomy through their conflicts with the adult world. Parent's willingness to struggle is itself more important than winning and losing.

(9) Finally, parents need to be reminded that adolescence is not a terminal disease and that most kids grow up in spite of themselves. Parents also need to be reminded that they are

human, make mistakes, routinely forget all the good advice listed above, and are simply "holding on for dear life."

Frequently, parents are too disempowered to effectively set any limits. I encourage them simply to stop fighting so many losing battles with their kids. The parents need to gain control over their helpless reactivity to the child's rebellious behavior. I want them to take charge of their not being in charge. I often ask them to write a letter that basically acknowledges their powerlessness. The following is a letter written to one 16-year-old boy by his parents.

Dear Daniel,

It must be obvious to you that we have been completely unable to get you to accept our rules and authority as your parents. At this point, we feel that we simply cannot control you or protect you from continuing on a very self-destructive course.

We strongly believe that you are using drugs frequently. You have been skipping school and coming and going as you please. When we tell you that you have to be home at a certain time, you just ignore us, and when we attempt to ground you, you just walk out and go to a friend's house to stay for a couple of days.

Daniel, we are scared for you. We feel that you are doing things that are dangerous and we cannot stop you right now. We love you. We wish we could protect you. We're going to work hard to learn how to reach you and help you get some control over yourself. But for now we're going to stop fighting with you all the time. It is not good for you or for us for there to be constant fighting about your behavior.

At this point you are basically a man. You have the power to wreck your life if you choose, but we will not give up trying to find a way to help you.

Love,

Mom and Dad

A letter such as this is not the answer, but at least it is a step toward helping "the tail stop wagging the dog."

Whenever possible in this stage of empowering parents, I encourage them to seek out support groups like Tough Love or Al-Anon in order to feel less isolated and overwhelmed by their problems with their adolescents. Too frequently these families live in complete isolation, and the parents feel too ashamed of their failings with their children to reach out to friends or relatives for support. Joining a group of other parents who are struggling with the same issues often brings a strong sense of relief to clients who suffer from the fear that they are all alone. I also tend to be quite open about my own concerns and frustrations about parenting, as another way of helping parents with their isolation and their shame.

The two key elements for empowering parents are for the therapist (1) to communicate to the parents that they represent the core of the solution rather than the cause of the problem and (2) to help them learn how to pick their battles carefully. Parents cannot truly control adolescents, but they can learn how not to be controlled by them.

Stage 4: The Crisis of Change

When the parents become a more effective and empowered team, a significant family crisis invariably results. Adolescents are similar to toddlers in their need to test limits strenuously before they accept them. This is particularly true when parents have changed their behavior as a result of therapy. The adolescent needs to challenge the change in order to find out if the parents are really committed to it and willing to follow through. It will not be enough for the parents to set limits with strong consequences. Invariably, adolescents will break the limit and attempt to avoid the consequence. Parents must be carefully prepared for this eventuality and have a series of alternatives in anticipation of the teenager's resistance. I find myself posing questions such as, "If he decides to test you by breaking curfew and when you ground him for a weekend he doesn't show up after school on Friday, then what are you going to do?"

Adolescents will test their parents' resolve either by flagrantly disobeying the rule and seeing if the parents have the will to impose the maximum consequence or by skillfully finding a little loophole in the rule and exploiting it. In the latter case the parents are left with the dilemma of choosing between imposing the consequence "unfairly" or backing off and acknowledging that the child was successful in finding a legitimate loophole. Some teenagers are able to see that contracts can be used to reduce parental control and scrutiny if the adolescent simply insists that the terms of the contract be taken literally.

It is at this point of crisis that the adolescent's level of dependency on chemicals becomes more clearly defined. As the parents and the other adults in the system become united and effective, kids who are only superficially involved with chemicals will tend to resist mightily and protest loudly, but their behavior will begin to improve and they will generally be able to accept limits. Teenagers who are in serious trouble with drugs and alcohol will not be able to change easily because they are not really in control. Thus, the crisis will escalate as the adolescent's inability to respond to parental limits becomes more apparent.

When this happens I begin to focus the family treatment on the likelihood that the teenager cannot respond to limits due to his being involved in hidden chemical dependency. I explain that it is not that the adolescent is unwilling to change; rather, he/she is no longer able to change. By introducing the disease model of addiction at this point, I am softening the scapegoating process that has become intensified by the parents' becoming more assertive. If the parents are setting limits and imposing consequences and the situation is simply becoming more out of control, then the disease model becomes a way of reframing the adolescent's behavior. This defuses the power struggle and provides the adolescent with a face-saving way of accepting parental control.

Introducing the idea that the adolescent is powerless over his behavior because he cannot handle his drug use often has a paradoxical effect. Many teenagers resist mightily the notion that they cannot control themselves and so set out to prove that they have no chemical dependency problem. The way to prove that they are not chemically dependent is to conform to the contracts that have been agreed upon; therefore, some adolescents begin to accept the contracts almost in spite of themselves.

However, most teenagers in serious trouble with chemicals cannot respond to this paradox. A direct confrontation of the substance abuse is usually in order. If there is clear-cut evidence of substance abuse, as well as friends and other concerned adults who know about the problem and willing to help, an intervention as described in Chapter 4 is extremely effective.

There are two elements to doing a successful intervention with adolescents. First, other teenagers whom the adolescent cares about and respects need to be involved. The impact of the adolescent's peers confronting the substance abuse is enormous, because so much of the substance abuse is intertwined with anxieties around peer relationships. When your friends tell you that they are worried about you and think that you have a problem, you're likely to take their warnings much more seriously than your parents' constant nagging. Secondly, it is very important to involve adults other than the parents. The voices of one or two caring adults who have no particular involvement in the power struggle between the parents and the adolescents will be heard over the parents' complaints during an intervention.

During this crisis period, whether an intervention is done or not, inpatient treatment becomes a possibility. I think a residential program that uses a solid therapeutic community model, is sophisticated about chemical dependency, and offers a strong family program for all family members is ideal for teenagers with serious chemical dependency, since there are so few resources and supports for abstinent adolescents in the community. Often the month of inpatient treatment, during which there is intensive peer support and encouragement to stay sober, is necessary to start adolescents on the road to recovery.

Family members need to learn how to handle the newly sober adolescent, who will seem like a stranger to them when he comes home. It is not unusual for kids to come out of residential programs with a fanatical commitment to their own sobriety and the values that they learned in the program. They are often intolerant of their parents and siblings who have not "dealt with their issues." The whole family needs to be educated about the recovery process and teenagers' appropriate need for rigidity about their sobriety. Family members need to develop new ways of relating rather than retreating toward the old pattern; otherwise they might end up scapegoating the adolescent who is now in recovery.

Residential treatment programs are effective when the adolescent is chemically dependent and when the parents themselves have so thoroughly lost control over the adolescent that they cannot protect the child from himself. However, if a program has already been tried and it has not been successful, then that usually indicates that there may be an underlying function to having the adolescent in the scapegoat role that is actively being reinforced by inpatient treatment.

Parents who have viewed their adolescent as "bad" are often relieved by shifting their perception to seeing their child as "sick." That reframe may break the impasse. Unfortunately, many families too readily identify their child as "sick" and are quite comfortable about turning the child over to the doctors and the inpatient program to be cured. These families tend to use the "sick" label to avoid putting pressure on the adolescent to be responsible for himself and to get caught in helpless enabling behavior. In these situations repeat hospitalizations protect the family from actually letting go of the child. The old family pattern is perpetuated, with the hospital becoming an unwitting partner in maintaining a dysfunctional homeostasis.

With some inpatient programs that work specifically with chemically dependent teenagers a new difficulty sometimes arises. The treatment staff may be too ideologically committed to the family disease model of addiction. This can lead them to confront parents on their own "disease" in a way that alienates rather than joins. If parents are challenged too early in the treatment process, they will sabotage the treatment and the child's recovery.

When the adolescent is older, i.e., in the late teens or twenties, or when residential programs have already been tried, the crisis-of-change stage may involve supporting the parents through difficult tasks. They must resist rescuing the abuser by simply putting him/her into inpatient treatment. Further, they must become powerful enough and detached enough to simply set limits, with the ultimate consequence being that the child can no longer live at home or be supported by the parents. The parents must state to the adolescent that they will be supportive if the abuser seeks treatment on his own but that initiating and following through with treatment are his responsibilities.

At this critical juncture, when the parents are faced with having to tell their out-of-control adolescent that he can no longer live at home or be supported by them, the situation becomes very scary. Almost always, when the parents are able to take such a strong position, the kid will escalate the level of defiance to the point of threatening to harm himself or members of the family.

Mr. and Mrs. Harris finally decided to stand up to their 25-year-old heroin-addicted son, Alan. It had taken them a long time to genuinely believe that kicking him out of the house was necessary and that letting him continue to stay dependent on them was like putting junk in his veins. They had already forced Alan into three hospitalizations, so they bascially knew that there was no other choice. They were just scared.

The first weekend after they told him to leave home, Alan found a exquisite way of trying to undermine their will to hold firm. Many times during the weekend he went to various subway stations, chose a phone close to the tracks, and called his folks. When they answered the phone he wouldn't say anything. He would simply hold the phone out towards the tracks, so that the parents could hear the rumble of the trains going by. Then he would say into the phone in a harsh whisper, "I'm going to throw myself in front of the next train that comes in because that's what you want. You want to get rid of me. Thanks." Then he would hang up before the parents could say anything.

It was a long, long weekend. The parents were scared and so was I. We knew he was capable of doing what he was threatening. There was nothing to be done. On Monday he signed himself into detox and for the first time took responsibility for his own recovery.

That case worked out. Some don't. Parents are not simply pathological, resistant, or stupid when they cannot confront their children. They're scared and they know that it is a matter of life and death. I don't want to be the one who aggressively pushes the parents in this crisis-of-change stage, because they ultimately have to be prepared to hold the line and take the consequences of what might happen. I spend a considerable amount of time helping parents prepare for this confrontation and appreciating their fears. The parents are ready for the crisis when they truly believe that continuing on the current path will lead to permanent disablement and possible death and that confronting the child may be the only way to help him.

Stage 5: Restraint from Change

After the family has successfully gone through the crisis stage and the adolescent is functioning much better in terms of both chemical use and behavior, we enter a somewhat awkward stage. The family continues to come into treatment and yet no one knows what to talk about. The sessions begin with family members' descriptions of how much better the identified patient is; then there is a period of mutual congratulations. Yet before long the conversation becomes strained and the tension level in the room begins to rise. At first everyone seems to feel the warm, soothing glow that one might have while drinking a cup of hot soup after being out on a cold winter's day. Then you can almost hear the "dum, dum, dum" of the theme music from the movie *Jaws*. You can almost see a black fin circling around ominously in the cup of nice, hot soup.

The shark in the soup represents all the unresolved issues, conflicts, and secrets that have not been addressed in the therapy because the family members have been devoting their attention to the scapegoat. Just as in the early stages of recovery for one of the parents, they do not know how to interact now that the crisis has passed and the adolescent is better. This stage is particularly awkward because there is tension around the underlying question: Should the therapy move on to address other family or marital problems? There is also considerable confusion about how best to relate to the recovering adolescent.

Usually in these session following the adolescent's improvement, when no one is quite sure what the topic of the therapy should be, one of the parents inadvertently broaches a new issue. Often this has to do with a significant marital or individual problem. Almost before he or she realizes it, the unwary therapist is working on topics that have never been agreed upon as part of the therapy and that some members of the family may actively resist discussing.

Suddenly Mrs. Jones wants to talk about how Mr. Jones only pays attention to her when there is a crisis in the family. Now that Bobby is better Mr. Jones is ignoring her again. Mr. Jones responds defensively. Then there is abruptly a marital argument in the room. Mrs. Jones turns to the therapist for help and requests some sessions for the couple to work on their relationship. Clearly Mr. Jones does not like the idea and the kids look uncomfortable.

Perhaps by the next session Bobby will have created a crisis again and this talk of marital therapy will be swept away.

During this strained transitional stage I strongly encourage the family to resist the temptation to move on to other issues. It is important to stay focused on the every day mechanics of recovery without expecting that longstanding family disputes will be opened up and resolved. While appreciating the wish of some family members to address other problems, I keep the work focused on the adolescent and his recovery until the family has sustained a solid period of stability without relapses. As in the Carey case, (Chapter 6), I make explicit the possibility that, if we move too quickly to other issues in the system, the adolescent may take it upon himself to rescue the family by getting into trouble again.

While restraining the family from moving on to other issues, I go through many of the same steps that I do when working with the alcoholic couple system. I work with each member of the family in the presence of the others around adjustment difficulties. I teach family members how to negotiate and manage conflict. We address the family's grief over the time lost to the struggle with the adolescent.

Adolescents go through this stage of recovery in two quite different ways. Some, particularly those who are coming out of intensive residential treatment centers, return to the family with a reformer's zeal. They feel that their recovery is dependent on the other family members' acknowledgment that they, too, are "sick" and need to be in recovery. Naturally, other family members may resist this idea. I actively support the adolescent's zeal in terms of his/her own recovery. Then, without overtly criticizing his efforts to reform the family, I encourage him to let the family members come along at their own pace and not to risk his own recovery by becoming too involved in theirs. I usually communicate this perspective through the language and teachings of AA and Al-Anon ("one step at a time"; "easy does it"; "don't take other people's inventory") The wish to change the whole family is also in part an expression of adolescent's unresolved grief as he begins to face the possibility that the family will not ever be the way he or she would like it to be and that it is time to leave the family behind.

The second typical pattern is one of occasional relapses. It is important that neither the parents nor I get overly excited by relapses. I normalize them as part of the adolescent's continuing effort to become more autonomous and learn by making mistakes. I encourage the parents to practice what they learned earlier in the therapy around setting limits and enacting consequences. I hypothesize in their presence that the adolescent is not feeling sufficiently grown up to be completely successful and needs the slips to keep the parents involved. I also hypothesize that perhaps the adolescent does not feel that the family is ready to have him be completely retired from the scapegoat position. What issues will they have to deal with if the adolescent is no longer center stage? The key to managing relapses is to block the event from completely dominating the family and to keep the parents from returning to their previous crisis mentality in their responses.

Regardless of whether the adolescent is overly zealous or caught in a relapse pattern, continuing involvement in support groups such as AA or Al-Anon is essential. I also encourage the families to practice having meetings on their own to address ongoing family problems, rather than relying on the therapy as the only place to talk. I begin to space out the meetings, so that the family members come to rely more on themselves and support systems in their community. To ensure success, they need to develop confidence that they can handle crises on their own without the therapist.

Stage 6: Individuation

When the family members are feeling more independent and competent, it is time for a shift in the focus of the therapy. Even though the adolescent is doing well, he may still have some developmental issues that he would like to work on without his parents' involvement. Kids who have been preoccupied with being symptomatic and the center of family turmoil often have not had the opportunity to address normal adolescent confusion and anxiety about self-image, sexuality, future planning, and peer relationships.

The goal of the last stage of therapy is to enable family members to individuate and facilitate the adolescent's autonomy and independence. The adolescent is encouraged to work individually on his own personal issues. In order to maintain my alliance with the whole family and ensure the adolescent's privacy, I usually refer the teenager to an individual therapist at this stage. If the adolescent chooses to handle developmental issues the way that most adolescents do (that is, the trial and error method) I encourage the parents to back off and try not to be controlling. This is particularly important if the adolescent is living at home, but old enough to be considered an adult — 17 or older. The parents and the adolescent have to negotiate the difference between the parents' asserting their rights as the providers of food and shelter and their attempting to impose their values and standards. It needs to be made clear that the adolescent has the right to reject the parents' rules or values as long as he/she is willing to be self-supporting and find his/her own place to live. Thus, the issue is defined as the negotiation of "boardinghouse rules" rather than a parent-child struggle over values and lifestyles.

Not only is the adolescent focusing on his individual issues and separating himself from the family, but the parents are also having to address the underlying issues of letting the child go, accepting him for who he is rather than who they wanted him to be, and beginning to face their own relationship as a couple. Making this transition to the marital issues is often a very delicate process. As I encourage the adolescent to deal with developmental issues independently of the family, I gently open up the marital relationship by encouraging the parents to reward themselves for having worked so hard at this difficult process. Perhaps, I say, they might try an activity that would not involve the children. This rather benign suggestion often reveals the lack of connection and intimacy between the parents that has been covered over by their struggle around the adolescent's behavior.

I want to make it safe for the couple to address marital issues in the therapy, but I do not want to push too hard. It is not my place to decide whether spouses should or should not use therapy as the way to readjust their marriage as the children begin to leave home. All couples go through considerable stress at this point and most of them weather the storm without therapy. Rather than push marital therapy, I normalize the transitional difficulties and make explicit the possibility that the adolescent may have a relapse in order to protect them from focusing too intensely on their couple relationship.

If spouses decide they would like to work on their marriage with me, I point out that here are several steps to go through to ensure that the family is really ready to handle the change in focus. First I want the family members to have a successful recess from therapy, in order to enhance their self-confidence in their abilities to manage problems. Secondly, I want to be sure that both spouses want to pursue marital therapy. Frequently one really wants the therapy and the other is going along with the idea to placate the spouse. Finally, I want the parents to explain to the kids that, even though there may be increased tension between them as they do the therapy, they would really like the kids to stay out of trouble and not to rescue them by creating diversionary crises. These preliminaries both prepare the parents for the normal tensions of marital therapy and block the return of the symptom. During the individuation stage the therapist becomes less central. As I have mentioned in previous chapters, in such an active and directive therapy it is a complicated task for the therapist to effectively disengage. Crises that happen during this late stage of therapy are usually related to the family's anxiety about losing the therapist. Individuation is hard for everybody in the treatment system, including me. It is hard not to be needed anymore.

NECESSITY IS THE MOTHER OF INVENTION

How does one translate generic treatment models into actual clinical situations? Models are never more than the frameworks for thinking about a family system and a preliminary way of organizing treatment. Each family is unique; ultimately every therapy is different. Treating adolescent substance abuse often means confronting life-threatening situations. Sometimes such desperate circumstances demand desperate responses.

As in the following case, sometimes I need to let go of my neat formulas and pat strategies and simply trust my intuition that doing something is safer than doing nothing.

It was the first session. The parents, Mr. and Mrs. Moss, were sitting close together on the sofa, wringing their hands and looking at me anxiously. The "child," Patrick, was a rude, foul-mouthed, 19-year-old adolescent who responded to most of my questions by swearing under his breath while refusing to answer directly. When I encouraged the parents to confront Patrick they looked at me with abject terror, as if I had just asked them to jump out of an airplane without a parachute.

It turned out that Patrick had been a drug addict for several years. He had been in inpatient treatment twice with no apparent success. As I tried to find out what the situation was at home, it quickly became apparent that the boy was running the show. About once every six weeks he would steal the family TV set and hock it for drug money. Then he would badger the parents into buying a new one. When the parents searched his room and found drugs they would flush the drugs down the toilet. He would simply replace the drugs in the exact same hiding places. Mr. and Mrs. Moss ran a small travel agency together. Naturally Patrick worked for them and just as naturally he stole money out of petty cash on a daily basis.

By the end of the interview I was feeling quite overwhelmed by these helpless parents and their difficult child. As the parents and I were discussing the possibility of another interview, the boy turned to them and said, "This shit is a waste of my fuckin' time. I don't care how much money you pay me, I'm not coming back to one of these stupid things." At this point I found out that the boy had been paid twice as much as I was being paid for the session. That information helped me understand why I felt so powerless throughout the interview. It is always a good idea to get paid more than the identified patient!

I decided that my first major intervention would be to tell the parents that they should either pay me twice as much as Patrick for our sessions or not pay him at all. The boy resolved the dilemma by stomping out of the room.

The therapy was launched in this rather shaky manner, and the following sessions were not a great improvement. Patrick didn't return and the parents took turns undermining any suggestions on my part that involved challenging their "poor sick" son. They had decided that he was ill and therefore they couldn't confront him. After all, he was not responsible for his behavior. They also carefully explained to me that they could not set limits on Patrick because obviously he was too big to be punished; further, they could not throw him out of the house because then he would get arrested and sent to jail, where he might get in "serious trouble." I was beginning to feel a little exasperated.

In session seven a significant shift in the therapy took place. This was precipitated by the boy's once again lifting the family TV set. The parents were desperately upset and turned to me to save their son. I was beginning to see that I had been pushing them too hard. They needed to find a response to this boy that genuinely empowered them and yet did not scare them so much that they couldn't do it. Clearly they were not ready to confront the boy directly, but they were desperate and said they would do anything I told them to do. I gave them the following four homework assignments.

(1) Mrs. Moss was instructed to get up one morning at 3 and cook Patrick an elaborate breakfast in bed. Then she was to carry the tray into his room, turn on the lights, wake him up, and put the tray gently on his chest. She was to greet him with a big smile and announce that she loved him so much that she just couldn't resist the urge to make him breakfast in bed.

(2) Mr. and Mrs. Moss were encouraged to go all over the house finding the boy's hiding places for drug. Instead of removing the drug, they were to leave in each place a note that said, "Surprise! Old dogs *can* learn new tricks."

(3) The father was encouraged to pick up a bunch of crisp new $10 bills from the bank. Each day he was to leave one of the bills around the office; attached to it would be a note saying, "Don't spend it all in one place."

(4) The mother was told to fill up the refrigerator with jars of baby food. When her son asked her what the jars were doing in the refrigerator, she was to say, "Well, you never know when we might have a new little someone around here." (This last intervention, an apparent flight of fancy, was related to my knowing that the boy was the youngest of two adopted children and my being struck with how comfortable he was with being the permanent baby of the family.)

The parents were somewhat perplexed by these ideas, but they were quick to acknowledge that conventional strategies had already failed and they did not have a lot to lose. They were also clearly intrigued with the possibility that for once Patrick would not be calling all the shots.

The change in the parents at the next interview was quite dramatic. They had done all the assignments and thoroughly enjoyed their son's bewilderment and discomfort. Their son has become quite upset and accused the parents of being crazy. He also told them that their "shrink" was crazy and should be fired. Feeling united and empowered, the parents decided that it was time Patrick either went into treatment on his own or lived somewhere else. I was very pleased and, I might add, very impressed with my "moves."

I should have known better. A week later the parents called me at 11 o'clock at night. They were hysterical. The mother said, "We did what you told us, Dr. Treadway. We kicked him out of the house and told him he could not come back in the house for nine months."

(I always get nervous when people call at 11 o'clock at night to tell me that they did what *I* told them to do.)

Mrs. Moss went on to explain that Patrick's response was to go out in the middle of this cold December night in his shirtsleeves, with the intent of freezing himself to death in front of their living-room picture window. The parents didn't know what to do. They didn't want to back down on their position. They did not want to call the police and have him dragged off the lawn. They thought he might just be stubborn enough and stoned enough to freeze himself to death.

I didn't know what to do. None of my treatment models prepared me for front lawn suicides. After some hesitation I told the parents to cajole their son into spending the night in the family car. I encouraged them to take turns sitting in the car with the boy, but not to allow him to talk them into letting him come back into the house. I encouraged the mother to make some coffee and take some blankets out to the car. It took some work, but eventually the parents were able to get their son into the car, where they took turns staying with him.

At 7 o'clock in the morning I arrived at their house to do an emergency session. You might wonder why I didn't insist that the family come to my office. The truth is that I was quite rattled by this turn of events. Naturally, we met in the car. I had Mom and Dad in the front seat, in the proper hierarchical position; Patrick and I were in the back seat. By this time he was cold sober and convinced that his parents and I were out of our minds. When it sunk in that the parents were serious about not letting him live in the house, he opted to put himself in the hospital.

After two weeks in the hospital, he called his parents and announced that he was cured and willing to come home as long as they fired me. Without consulting me, the parents told him that, although they wanted to see him and were encouraged about his treatment, they would neither support him nor allow him back into their home for eight months and two weeks.

The son ended up going through an extended inpatient rehabilitation program. When he completed it, he found a job and place to live in a neighboring state. I continued to see the parents for a while for check-up sessions. They went on their first vacation together in 12 years.

At the eight-month mark the son called the parents and told them he had a girlfriend and would like to bring her home to meet the folks. The parents told him that they thought this was great news, but suggested that they either meet in a restaurant or postpone the visit for another month.

Sometimes old dogs can learn new tricks. Even therapists.

8

Healing the Wounds, Living with the Scars: Working with Adult Children of Alcoholics

Jim likes sports. He knows all the players on all the teams. He marks the seasons by the rotation of sports on TV rather than the change in weather. He works hard and wants to be a good husband and father, but in actuality he feels best when he's alone and there is a good game on.

Cindy complains that she has to initiate everything. She says Jim never pays any attention to her and that all he ever wants to talk about is sports. Jim feels that Cindy is angry all the time. He doesn't understand why she is always complaining that he doesn't meet her needs.

Jim and Cindy don't make love anymore. They just never seem to have the time. They don't fight about it. Jim is never "in the mood." He doesn't know why merely the idea of being sexual makes him feel anxious. Cindy avoids the subject. She complains about other things instead. They don't go to bed at the same time. They never touch. They seem to have an understanding about not "rocking the boat."

Jim was six when he learned that his mother wouldn't notice him if he slipped up the stairs and went into his room. He would stay up there for hours listening to the ballgames on the radio. Sometimes he would even be able get away with skipping dinner. As his mother's drinking got worse, he found that he could get through a whole day and not be on the receiving end of any of her tirades. He made sure that he was never in the same room with her. She stopped noticing his absence. Jim felt guilty about his brother who never learned how to stay out of Mom's way.

Cindy has nightmares about being smothered. She can't stand the smell of alcohol. She doesn't remember much about her childhood except her Mom and Dad's late night fights. Her Dad would come home drunk, wake up her mother, and start yelling at her about what a cold, frigid bitch she was. Then her father would come into Cindy's room, drag her out of bed, and make her listen to his tirades about her mother. He would lecture her about how she better not turn out like her mother. When she complained about these outbursts to her mother, her mother told her not to worry about them. "Men are just like that," she said. Cindy used to daydream about growing up and falling in love with a different kind of man.

*   *   *   *   *

The story seems too pat. The links between the past and the present seem so obvious. Yet when Jim and Cindy came into my office they didn't have any sense that their childhood experiences had any relationship to their marital problems. It took time to uncover the old wounds. Nobody escapes childhood unscathed, but children growing up in alcoholic family systems bear heavier scars than most. The very survival strategies that helped them manage the chaos of growing up often become major impediments to successfully engaging in adult relationships.

Most ACOAs are unaware of the relationship between their early life experiences growing up in a dysfunctional family and the problems that bring them into treatment. Yet, due to the legacy of low self-esteem, difficulties with trust, unresolved dependency, and blocked affect, adult children are likely to develop a wide variety of symptoms. In addition to being at very high risk for replicating the alcoholic family system by becoming an alcoholic, marrying one, or parenting one, ACOAs are particularly vulnerable to having difficulties in their close relationships.

A strong fear of being hurt and a desire for nurturance are usually the prime motivating forces for ACOAs in their relationships. For most ACOAs, these needs for safety and for intimacy are mutually exclusive. Intimacy is based on the partners' being trusting, affectively available, and interdependent. For the adult child this is a very unsafe position, one that almost always evokes the sense of danger, dread, and entrapment from childhood.

ACOAs struggle often unconsciously to find a form of intimacy that doesn't sacrifice safety. Many adult children simply avoid becoming too close to others, preferring a life alone to the risks of being hurt in a close relationship. Others find ways to engage in self-protective partial intimacy. They may find emotional closeness acceptable, but sexual intimacy impossible or vice versa. They may become emotional pursuers, thereby avoiding the anxiety of waiting to be sought after. Alternatively, they may play the role of distancer, avoiding the risk of rejection. Some individuals manage by maintaining multiple relationships, rather than putting all their emotional eggs in one basket.

The need for safety is compounded by the fact that adult children usually are blocked affectively and have very little underlying self-esteem. This leads them to be unaware of how they are expressing their anxiety and neediness in relationships as well as afraid that everything is their fault in the first place. Adult children are prone to remain in abusive relationships because they are not in touch with feeling abused and feel that they don't deserve any better.

Finally, ACOAs seek in their present relationships a chance to make up for their past pain. They may look to marry strong competent people who, they hope, will be able to take care of them in a way that didn't happen in their childhood. Conversely, they may marry underfunctioning spouses, since they feel most comfortable in the caretaker role. Such a marriage gives them a chance to rewrite the story. The young woman may not have been able to rescue her alcoholic father, but maybe she can transform this rebellious young man with her love.

Seeking in one's adult relationships emotional reparations for the hurts of childhood is an effort doomed to failure. No matter how much the spouse loves the ACOA, he/she can't really make up for the past and will often feel inadequate. Spouses become frustrated and tend to distance because they feel that nothing they do is ever good enough. This response only confirms the ACOAs' worst fear, which is that other people will ultimately abandon them.

FOUR-STAGE TREATMENT MODEL

Stage 1: Engage in the Present; Assess the Past

We start by accepting the clients' presenting problem while engaging the couple in the treatment.

Traditional individual psychotherapy can be intensely difficult for ACOAs for three main reasons: (1) The nondirective style makes the therapy feel confusing and unsafe; ACOAs cannot handle the performance anxiety experienced when they do not understand what is expected of them. (2) The emphasis on expressing feelings may make the ACOA feel like failures because they are often thoroughly blocked affectively and literally don't know what they feel much less how to express it. (3) Finally, the transference process often induces a strong regressive tendency. Since the therapy relationship replicates the child-parent relationship, ACOAs tend to experience considerable anxiety about whether to allow themselves to trust and become dependent on the therapist. If ACOAs do decide to trust the therapist, they may give up their defenses precipitously and overwhelm the therapist with their lifelong unmet dependency needs. As the therapist quite naturally attempts to set limits on their needs and expectations, ACOAs are likely to experience the therapist as being rejecting and inconsistent, e.g. "just like my father." This confirms the wisdom of ACOAs' oldest defense, which is that ultimately no one is trustworthy. At this critical juncture when the therapist is trying to work through the transference issue, many ACOA's are likely to abruptly end treatment.

Clearly many skilled therapists are able to work through this process with their clients and to use the transference issues effectively. However, many ACOAs whom I have encountered, have experienced their individual therapy as a harsh reenactment of their childhood. When the therapy was going badly, they felt that it was all their fault. Consequently, I prefer to begin with the couple or the family and define problems interactionally; this gives me a chance to assess the function of the problem, the clients' strengths, and the utility of their defenses within their own idiosyncratic system.

Although it is useful for me to identify in my own mind the connection between the presenting problem and clients' unresolved issues from the family of origin, I do not push the ACOA issue prematurely. ACOAs come into treatment secretly afraid that they have caused the relationship problem. If I introduce the ACOA concept right away, they may feel blamed instead of supported. For example, if a woman has initiated marital therapy, she may feel criticized if I introduce the ACOA perspective in order to explain her part of the marital problem. I don't begin therapy with history. I begin with affirmation and with defining manageable interactional problems in the present. When treating ACOAs, the message is quite simple: Build them up before opening them up.

In terms of assessment, I am always aware of the possibility of a link between the presenting problems and unresolved ACOA issues in one or both of the adults. The key, however, is to find ways to assess the family-of-origin issues without being too threatening. I keep the questions focused on the presenting problem while opening the lens to include three generations. If I'm treating an individual symptom, I may naturally ask: Who else in your family has had problems like this? If it is a marital problem, then I ask: How does your marriage compare to your parents'? If a child is the presenting problem, I ask: How did your parents (the grandparents) handle this kind of a problem when you were a kid? What do you want to do with your children differently from what your parents did with you? These questions elicit information about the family of origin and lead me to hypothesize about the relationship between the ACOA issues and the presenting problem. The questions themselves help individuals develop awareness of the links between the presenting problems and the family-of-origin issues. The trick is to keep these emerging links to myself, even if the connections seem obvious, because I don't want to rush ahead of my clients.

I do not assume that I will have to work on the ACOA issues in order to treat the case effectively. Many clients have defenses that work quite well for them; they may need only a slight adjustment around managing the presenting problem. People by and large do not come into treatment to be cured of everything that ever happened to them. It's my job to help them fix what they want to get fixed. Just because individuals like Cindy and Jim come from dysfunctional families does not mean that they are asking to be treated for it.

The initial stage of therapy with ACOAs tends to look like the beginning of any couples therapy. I encourage clients to define the problems and begin to work on them. Some couples will be able to resolve their issues relatively easily with some negotiation and coaching. However, when the presenting problem proves to be intractable and the clients feel stuck, it becomes useful to open up the broader connections between family-of-origin issues and the couple's relationship problems.

Stage 2: Restraint from Change

Couples like Jim and Cindy come into therapy wanting to have a closer, more intimate relationship, and yet they don't really know what prevents that. By the time they reach my office they have accumulated a series of painful defeats, in which each has tried in his or her own way to bridge the gap. Invariably, both feel rejected, hurt, and helpless, regardless of whether they blame themselves or the partner.

After the initial steps of joining the spouses and making the therapy feel safe, I open up the past more explicitly as a way of understanding their present impasse. After Cindy describes being abused by her father's tirades, it becomes easier for Jim to understand and accept Cindy's difficulties with trust and need for reassurance. By the same token, Cindy can appreciate Jim's passivity and lack of interest in sex once she has a picture of his vulnerable position with his domineering mother and his need to protect himself.

In almost all couples cases, the initial stage of treatment involves defusing the blame game and helping spouse gain greater empathy and understanding of the partner. Introducing the family-of-origin issues is a way of helping spouses accept each other's differences instead of struggling over which one of them is right. Opening up the past softens their anger and defensiveness with each other and allows them to reconnect; however it also makes them vulnerable to each other. The combination of reducing the level of conflict and bringing up the emotional pain of the past creates a volatile moment when neither spouse feels particularly safe. The familiar rituals for maintaining distance through conflict have been interrupted. At this critical juncture, their first tentative efforts to risk becoming closer often backfire because of their vulnerability and mistrust. At this point, I often recommend that they resist trying to change precipitously. At the end of the second interview, I gave Jim and Cindy the following restraint-from-change intervention, which I call "The Lobster Tale."

D.T.   Have I told you about how lobsters grow?

JIM   No, we haven't covered that yet.

D.T.   Well, lobsters grow by becoming too big for their old shells and then shedding them. They go through a very vulnerable period when they have shed the old shell but have not yet grown a new one. During this delicate transition they become inactive and essentially hide among the rocks while waiting for the new shell to grow.

The therapy room here needs to be a safe place where you can let go of your old shells and be protected while giving the new ones time to grow. It is a period to be inactive and not expect too much from each other.

You two have opened up a lot in this meeting and I'm hoping you won't try to do too much too soon. I'm worried, Jim, that you'll think that you should suddenly be able to be responsive in the bedroom. And Cindy, I have a feeling that you may be surprised to discover that it is uncomfortable for you when Jim starts making overtures. You may discover that you have a lot of distrust built up; you may even resent his trying to get closer.

Here's what I would like you to do between now and when I see you again. I would like you to agree *not* to have any sex, even if you both feel like it, because at this point I think both of you could easily be hurt by the other one's anxiety about it.

What I would like you to do, Jim, is write Cindy a note saying that you understand that she shouldn't pay for your mother's sins and that you're willing to work hard to rid your home of your Mom's shadow but that you will need Cindy's help, patience, and understanding. And Cindy, I want you to write Jim and explain to him that he shouldn't try and change too quickly because it will probably take you a long time to regain your trust anyway. You need to help him understand how humiliated you were by your Dad and how it's easier for you not to trust men or get close to them.

Lastly, I would like you to come to the next session with a list of fears you both might have about getting more intimate. Given how badly hurt you were as kids by the people you were closest to, you would be a little crazy if you didn't have some healthy fear about getting close and trusting each other. As kids you learned to take care of yourselves in the only way you knew how. You both grew pretty hard shells. It takes time to grow new ones that will fit better.

I'm not sure whether Jim's response meant that I had succeeded too well in restraining them from change, but it gave us all a laugh. He said, "Fine, now that you have us imagining that we're a couple of cold, wet, naked lobsters we will probably never get together in the bedroom."

All couples are torn between the wish to change and fear of the vulnerability that change creates. I help couples appreciate their fear and the risks of change. By restraining them from changing too quickly, I am putting myself in the protective role of helping them maintain a safe distance. This allows them to shed some of their own protective mechanisms for avoiding closeness, such as fighting, sexual avoidance, and lack of communication.

Any restraint from change intervention must be empathic and make sense to the clients. Restraint suggestions that do not make sense can be offensive, since most clients come to therapy with a conscious desire to change. They may feel misunderstood or even insulted if the therapist implies that they don't "want" to change or that they "need" to keep their problems. Watzlawick, Weakland, Fisch, and the rest of their MRI colleagues have been most outspoken about the salutory effects of interrupting people's entrenched and ineffective problem-solving behavior as a way of releasing the potential for change. I use this gentle restraint-from-change message to spouses who are "trying" to get closer to take the pressure off and allow them to feel safe enough to risk more openness and ultimately more intimacy.

Restraint-from-change moves don't necessarily work by themselves in therapy, but they will reduce some of the spouses' frustration, anxiety, and anger about their difficulties in resolving the presenting problems.

Stage 3: Supportive Exploration of Affect

If my clients allow themselves to open up to the painful feelings from their childhoods, they may experience intense reactions. Very competent and successful people will suddenly seem to be coming apart at the seams as they get in touch with the hurt and vulnerable child of many years ago. When ACOAs give up some of their primary defenses, such as denial, projection, and addictive behavior, they frequently experience either anxiety attacks or bouts of depression. They are truly like lobsters without their shells.

Before opening up the repressed affect that most ACOAs have about their past, I spend considerable time educating clients about the natural history of growing up in an alcoholic family, the roles people develop, and the healthy ways that children survive. It is very important that ACOAs appreciate the defenses and survival skills they developed as children. It is also important for spouses to appreciate their partners' defenses. I work hard at helping Cindy understand why Jim needed to sneak off to his room to listen to the ballgame and be alone. I also help Jim develop an empathic connection to what it was like for Cindy to be intimidated over and over again by her father. Cindy's yearnings for a man "different" from her father and Jim's need for protective isolation were part of how they survived their childhoods, but the two defenses collide in their marriage.

I also help each spouse distinguish between being responsive and being responsible. Most spouses of ACOAs feel overwhelmed and inadequate in response to their partners' needs. Ultimately they become discouraged and withdraw. I want the spouses to learn how to be empathic without feeling that they have to make up for the past. Spouses need to learn how to be supportive; their partners need to accept the limitations of their support. Love does not conquer all.

At this juncture I help the couple look outside the marriage for additional support. The ACOA literature and the many available

ACOA groups and workshops are useful in helping both spouses feel a sense of support, belonging, and normality about their shameful past and the scars they carry into the present. The group support is often essential in helping clients tolerate the flooding into consciousness of years of blocked affect. Just as Al-Anon and AA are essential in the successful treatment of active alcoholism, adult children groups have proven to be valuable in helping adult children come to terms with their past.Naturally, most ACOAs are reluctant to engage in any kind of group experience. I encourage reluctant clients to consider a professionally-led group first, because there they may feel safer than in the ACOA/Al-Anon groups. The leader will be skilled enough to help clients overcome their initial anxiety.

I have in the past few years run several retreats for adult children of alcoholics. These have been profoundly moving experiences, as people who have felt isolated in the world and filled with a sense of shame have finally experienced understanding and acceptance. One man said at the end of the weekend, "I feel like I've been welcomed home."

As emotional needs are opened up and the ACOA is supported in exploring the past, expectations of the marriage become less intense. The focus shifts to the family of origin. There is, nevertheless, a payoff in the marriage: This reduction of expectation often means that the spouse feels less pressure and is more responsive and forthcoming. Thus, in most cases, the spouse who expects less gets more.

Adult children of alcoholics come into treatment with a set of fixed responses to their past. They are usually angry, sad, or numb. Many ACOAs have arrived at a kind of pseudo-resolution. They often say that they "understand" that their parents "did the best they could" and that "it was nobody's fault in the end." This quite healthy defense covers over all the appropriate childhood feelings of anger and sadness, which are locked inside of the adult and played out unconsciously in his or her relationships.

Our task is to help the adult child to understand the range of feelings that are covered over by such set responses to the past and to see how those feelings inform and direct present behavior. Cindy "understood that her Dad was an alcoholic and had a 'disease'" without any awareness of how much she expressed her hurt and anger at her Dad in the way she attacked her husband. She said that she had no feelings at all when I asked her what it was like to be a little girl listening to her father's tirades. When I asked her to imagine how her daughter at the age of eight might feel if Jim came home drunk every night and dragged her out of bed to rail at her, Cindy could immediately see how her daughter would be over-whelmed, afraid, angry, confused, etc. Suddenly Cindy could see herself as a little girl instead of as a little grownup. She started to cry.

Helping clients acknowledge and even reexperience some of the charged affect from the past is usually the first step toward opening up the question of what they want to do about making peace with their family of origin. Until the emotion is brought to the surface, most ACOAs simply play out a rigid role vis-à-vis the family a role learned in childhood. Regardless of how unfulfilling their relation-ship to the family is, they dismiss both the hope and the need for change. Until clients have become comfortable with their pain and anxiety, they will be too anxious to attempt changing their roles and behavior in the family of origin.

Stage 4: Coming to Terms with the Past

Not all clients need to work through their relationships with their families of origin. Sometimes simply acknowledging the lega-cy of the past and its impact on the present is enough to allow spouses to become closer and more intimate. Many couples will be able to use the steps outlined in Chapter 5 on couples treatment to work through their conflicts and resolve their issues around sexual-ity and intimacy. I usually pursue active family of origin coaching when clients clearly see the link between their present problems and their past relationships, when they are motivated to change their position in the family of origin, and when the spouse is supportive.

I do not believe it is useful to ask clients to do family-of-origin work just on faith. I want clients to see that working on the past will help them change patterns of behavior that are hurtful to themselves and their partners in the present. Armor may have been appropriate protective outerwear in medieval England, but not in 20th-century America and particularly not with an intimate partner. ACOAs survived childhood by donning defensive armor, but those defenses have become suffocatingly cumbersome as well as obsolete in adult life. Going back to the family of origin makes sense if the client sees it as opportunity to take off the old armor and leave it behind.

I have three goals in mind when I encourage clients to address their family-of-origin issues. I want clients:

(1) To deepen their understanding of what happened growing up in their family, so that they can better understand themselves and the impact of their childhood on the present.

(2) To feel more empowered by taking charge of conducting their relationships with their parents and siblings, rather than remaining trapped in a helpless, reactive, one-down position.

(3) To accept the grief of recognizing that no one can make up for the past. Clients should not go into the family-of-origin work with the secret expectation that all their unmet needs of the past will be fulfilled and all their broken relationships healed.

The first step often involves helping clients disengage from the struggle to get from their parents or their siblings the validation, acceptance, and love they have always yearned for. Most ACOAs are in highly reactive relationships with their families. They painfully repeat their part of the old destructive patterns with little awareness of their behavior's impact. In order to break the pattern, they must recognize how their way of struggling is perpetuating the tug of war. I encourage them to take a "one-down" position, to give up trying either to change someone else or to win an old fight. Naturally, many of my clients argue with me about this, saying, "It's not fair that I should do all the work. It isn't right that my parent is being let off the hook." I respond, "It's true that it isn't fair, but if you're going to wait for it to be fair you're going to wait forever. The only way you can break this pattern with your folks is to be willing to do more than your share of the work."

Following are a couple examples of how I help clients "let go of the rope."

Jane was a very successful woman in her middle forties who ran a business and a household in an extremely competent way. As long as she was in control, she was loving, gracious, and generous; however she could not let anyone give to her. Jane and her husband fought about her controlling behavior and her inability to let him take the lead in any area in their lives. Jane knew that her behavior was getting in the way of her marriage. She could also see the roots of her behavior in her childhood. She had learned to manage living with a violent alcoholic mother after her Dad left when she was five. She avoided her mother's wrath as much as possible by becoming perfect. She never got less than an A in school, her clothes were always immaculate, and she conscientiously ran the household as her mother became progressively more disabled. Being in control kept her out of harm's way.

Once a year Jane felt compelled to make a dutiful visit to her mother, who was now a frail old lady. She had finally stopped drinking because of her health. Each year, as the time for the visit approached, Jane would be overcome with anxiety and discomfort. She would promise herself that she would keep the visit brief and not fight with her mother. Every year she would come home feeling awful. No matter how hard she tried not to fight with her mother, she simply couldn't stand how her mother treated her like an incompetent six-year-old and criticized everything she did. Jane would find herself compelled to defend herself, to prove she was a perfectly competent grown-up woman who didn't need to be told how to boil water or buy groceries. The mother would get mad, say things like "I was just trying to help," and then withdraw into a sulk. Jane would feel guilty and end up apologizing. The sequence had been going on this way for years.

D.T.   Well, Jane, it looks like your Mom is pretty good at getting you to act like a rebellious angry adolescent.

JANE   I do not act like an angry adolescent. That's a stupid thing to say!

D.T.   It seems to me that your Mom gets you running around the house saying, "I am grown-up! I am grown-up!". Now, I know you're a very successful, competent woman, so does your husband, so do your kids, so do your friends, and so do your employees. Why are you trying to prove it to some addle-brained little old lady in Georgia whom you see once a year?

JANE   I can't help myself. She makes me so mad.

D.T.   Try and think of it this way. You mother has wrecked her
  life and pickled her brain. She knows you can't stand her and
  she probably knows why. She sees what a success you've
  made out of your life and on some level she probably knows
  that she had nothing to do with it. Criticizing you is more
  than likely her way of making her feel less badly about
  herself, of expressing her jealousy, and dealing with her
  anger that you really don't want anything to do with her.
  She's never going to be the mother that you needed, Jane.
  She's never going to be the mother you deserved to have.
  She's just a pathetic old lady totally incapable of acting like
  an adult or accepting you as an adult.

JANE   (in tears) But I don't know what to do. I try so hard. You
  don't understand. She picks on everything I do.

D.T.   Well, Jane, here's what I would like to try. It may sound
  ridiculous, but I think it's a way that you can break your
  mother's spell and keep from getting caught in these fights
  with her. Are you willing to try something that's going to
  sound a little nuts?

JANE   I suppose.

D.T.   Well, you've got to tell me if this idea isn't right for you.
  Here it is. Whenever your mother is bossing you around and
  telling you what to do as if you were five years old, like
  telling you how to boil water or how to set the table, I would
  like you to say very gently and softly, almost under your
  breath, "Yes, Mommy," and then I want you to go off and do
  whatever she has told you do.

JANE   Why would I do that?

D.T.   Good question. Let me ask you one. What happens in a
  tug of war if one side lets go of the rope?

JANE   I guess the other side falls down.

D.T.   That's right. That's what you need to do with your
  mother. You need to take charge of this game. If you go
  out of your way to accept her bossing you around, she
  won't be able to pick a fight with you. Do you want to give it
  a try?

Jane decided to try it. We practiced in the office until she
could say " Yes, Mommy" without the slightest hint of sarcasm.
She and her husband also practiced at home. It wasn't long
before she was good at saying "Yes, Mommy" in a very sweet,
little girl voice.

She went off to Georgia for a two-week stay with her mother.

When she returned she reported that her mother constantly told her what to do and she constantly replied, "Yes, Mommy," and then went off and did whatever her mother said. Her mother was thrilled with her throughout the visit and never noticed the "Yes, Mommy." For the first time, they didn't have one fight during Jane's visit. As Jane went about being a "good girl" and doing what she was told, she was shocked to discover that she didn't feel at all abused by her mother's criticism. Instead she felt amused and in complete control. She was finally able to see that she really didn't need to prove herself to her mother. It wasn't her problem that her mother couldn't relate to her as an adult.

In the weeks following her success at "letting go of the rope" with her mother, Jane experimented with letting her husband be in charge of their love life and was surprised to discover how nice it felt to be on the receiving end of loving attention.

Ellen's alcoholic father had been suicidally depressed off and on since Ellen was a child. After her mother died, her father would call Ellen several times a week so that Ellen could cheer him up. Ellen, who is a social worker, would get engaged in lengthy phone conversations in which she would encourage her father to feel better about himself. By the end of these phone calls, the father seemed to feel better, but Ellen would be in a silent black rage. Inevitably she would lose her temper at either her husband or her children immediately after the call. She felt completely at the mercy of her father's depression.

I advised her to make a list of 20 empathic phrases she might have picked up in social work school, such as, "I am very sorry that you feel so badly," or "Tell me more," or "It must feel like nobody understands what you're going through." Then I encouraged her to stop allowing her father's calls to intrude on her life in a random fashion. She should take the initiative and call her father at a routine time each week. If her father called at other times, she could gently but firmly refuse to take the call. She was to prepare for her weekly call by planning a distraction for the kids, making herself a nice snack and a hot cup of tea, and sitting on the sofa with her husband and the list. She was to encourage her father to talk about his depression and see if she could insert into the conversation all 20 of her empathic statements. Once she finished the phone call, she was to talk a little with her husband about how difficult it had always been to feel responsible for her father and how much she wished her father would show some interest in her. Her husband was encouraged to let her have her feelings, no matter how despairing they were.

Ellen was quite resistant to this idea, because it seemed to her that I was trying to get her even more involved with her father. Much to her surprise she found that the calls to her father were shorter and that frequently she couldn't get her father to focus on being either depressed or suicidal. In one conversation, he actually asked why Ellen kept worrying about his being depressed and said there must be something else they could talk about. As Ellen checked off her empathic phrases, she and her husband shared a silent conspiratorial chuckle. No longer was Ellen's father able to drive a wedge between them; in fact, they were actually drawn together. She particularly liked his willingness to listen to her sadness about her father. He liked feeling it was okay to just listen rather than saying or doing something to make her feel better.

Learning how not to react to the old family patterns empowers the clients and makes them feel more in control of themselves and their relationships with members of their families of origin. They feel more confident that they can engage their family without being swallowed up in it. It is equally important for my clients to educate me about how their families work. When clients tell me that they can't do a given task, I accept their caution and assume that I have asked them to take too big a step. There is always a smaller step to be taken.

I once spent several months working with a client, helping him plan and initiate a luncheon with his Dad. He decided that the safest topic for discussion were the pennant hopes of the Boston Red Sox. We role played the initial phone call and the son antici-pated all the arguments his father would use in order to reject the lunch invitation. This preparation took a long time because the son had never initiated contact with his Dad before; he could not even remember having a conversation alone with his father. En-couraging this client to attempt a "meaningful" conversation with his Dad would have overwhelmed him. My client intuitively knew that, before he could have a serious conversation with his Dad, he needed to be able to have a successful superficial one.

I generally divide the family-of-origin work into four categories, working with (1) the siblings, (2) the alcoholic parent, (3) the co-dependent parent, and finally, (4) the child within. Although it is usually easiest to start with the siblings, I trust my clients' wisdom in making the choices. The clients' own instincts about what they and their family members can handle are usually the therapist's best guide.

Working with siblings. ACOAs tend to have two different types of sibling relationships. Some siblings are very close and talk frequently around their feelings about the family and its impact on them. These clients have little difficulty engaging their siblings in the therapeutic process. Most sibling relationships, however, are distant, competitive, and superficial. The siblings' feelings about their shared past are never discussed and they play out their old roles from childhood, e.g., hero, scapegoat, in highly ritualized patterns. In these situations the siblings don't see each other very often and rarely engage in anything more serious than small talk, except to fight with each other. Naturally, this kind of sibling relationship is protective, since the distance enables the siblings to avoid opening up the old pain around their experiences as children. Depending on which role they played, clients will feel either rejected by their siblings or resentful because they feel responsible for them.

Given the nature of these sibling relationships, it's not surprising that clients react to the idea of engaging their siblings with considerable fear of rejection and doubts about the potential value. Clients will make such comments as, "I've tried everything," or, "He's hopeless. All he cares about is making money." I accept that their fears are realistic and their resentments appropriate; however, I continue to encourage them to engage their siblings. There are three main reasons.

First, engaging their siblings on their own intiative empowers my clients and moves them out of the hurt, reactive, victim position. Secondly, learning about their siblings' perspective on what happened in the family helps my clients develop a broader perspective on their childhood and a more systemic understanding of the impact of alcoholism on the family. Siblings' versions of reality are often strikingly different; however, as with binocular vision, the different perspectives together increase depth perception. Finally, learning about the impact on their siblings of having grown up in an alcoholic family is normalizing. Frequently my clients, who are addressing the old wounds, are actually more at peace with themselves than their seemingly well-put-together brothers and sisters, who don't believe in "crying over spilled milk," "digging up the past," or "self-absorbed psychological ruminations."

I discourage clients from thinking that their needs for validation will be met by their siblings. What usually blocks communications between siblings about family of origin issues is tension around whose version of reality is more accurate. Clients have to be prepared not to push their own version or to challenge their sibling's story. They have to be willing to do more than their share of work, to meet on the other's terms, and to expect only minimal reciprocity of interest. I tell my clients that, even after they have worked hard to engage a sibling, they may in the end decide that the relationship is too uncomfortable to sustain. Ultimately they may return to the old level of distance. There is no mental health rule that states that siblings have to like each other or be close. These depressing caveats help my clients approach the sibling work with their eyes wide open.

Mary's older brother Charles, a stockbroker, would talk to her only about money and the stock market. Whenever she tried to talk with him about either her feelings or their shared experiences as children, he would rapidly change the subject to his latest financial undertaking or offer brotherly advice about how she should be protecting her assets. Mary sent him articles about ACOAs; he sent her clippings from the financial page. Mary and Charles had been extremely close as children; in fact, he had often protected her from their abusive father. Now Charles simply dismissed the past by saying there was no point in talking about it.

I coached Mary to begin shifting the relationship with her brother by asking him for advice in buying a few stocks. He was quite responsive, and they had many lengthy conversations about the management of her little portfolio. Mary began to see that this was Charles' way of taking care of her, just as he had done when they were kids, and she began to allow herself to enjoy his concern. After they worked together for several months on her financial status, Mary was able to get Charles to talk about growing up in their family. She explained to him that part of her family therapy training involved interviewing a sibling about their shared childhood. Charles was surprisingly willing to help on her "project."

Clients frequently tell me that their siblings are completely unable to talk to them about their feelings and memories about the past; in fact, they don't even acknowledge having feelings. However, once clients establish a working contact with a sibling, such as Mary did with Charles around the stock purchases, then they are able to open up the past. I coach clients to use factual and circular questions rather than questions about feelings. A brother who has no memories of the parents' fights may nevertheless remember his favorite toy, his best friend, or what they did when Dad lost his temper. A sister who says that there was nothing at all wrong in the family will still be able to answer such questions as: "Who was closest to Dad?" "Which of us kids got dragged into the middle of Mom and Dad's fights the most?" or "Of all of us, who do you think turned out most like Mom and who do you think is most like Dad?" Every sibling's story of what happened in the past is different; the true story is the composite portrait made up of everyone's different experiences.

One of my clients spent 30 years resenting her older sister because the sister was exempt from their father's beatings. After listening to her sister's shame and guilt about always being the favorite and watching the others being beaten, my client was finally able to see that although their experiences were different, they both bore the scars of growing up in an alcoholic family.

When the siblings are very close and have formed a kind of family within a family, it is easy to bring them together to talk about their experiences. It is particularly useful to have siblings who are open about their history talk about how it has affected their current life. For example, if a woman has difficulty forming trusting relationships with men, then it is useful to find out how her sister has handled relationships. Together they might explore a range of options and deepen their understanding about the aftereffects of having had a father who was dangerous.

As an outcome of the sibling work, my clients often better understand what happened in their family, better accept their siblings' ways of coping with the old wounds, and in many instances feel closer to their siblings. Sometimes the relationships change and are healed. Sometimes they are simply accepted for what they are.

Working with the alcoholic parent. There is a harsh scene in the movie, *I Never Sang For My Father*. The son is trying to make peace with his father, who has been a difficult, self-centered, and unapproachable man all of his adult life. Now the father is dying. In the scene, we see the son talking to the father about his longings for them to be closer, while the father sits on the sofa looking straight ahead. As the son asks for a response, the picture widens and we see the father lean forward and turn up the TV set.

People die as they have lived. Clients have to come to terms with the likelihood that their alcoholic parents will never fully understand or acknowledge the impact of their behavior on their children.

When I encourage clients to make contact with the alcoholic parent, I have three primary goals for them: (1) to develop an enhanced degree of power and autonomy in relationship to that parent; (2) to grieve the loss of the alcoholic parent and accept that, regardless of whether the alcoholic ever gets sober, nothing will ever completely make up for what happened in the past; and (3) to fully appreciate the disease process and to use that perspective in coming to terms with the destructive behavior of the alcoholic parent.

The necessary steps in coming to terms with an alcoholic parent will obviously vary depending on whether the parent is still actively drinking or in recovery and on whether he/she is still alive. If the alcoholic is still actively drinking, then the first step involves helping the client take more control over his/her interactions with the drinking parent. Many ACOAs are still enabling their parent's drinking behavior and have never directly confronted the drinker. I encourage my clients to explore the possibility of doing an intervention with their siblings; if that is not possible, they might consider doing their own confrontation (see Chapter 4 for a description of this process). This might mean that the ACOA openly confronts the alcoholic about the drinking for the very first time. One woman told her alcoholic father that he could no longer drive the car with her children in it because of her concerns about his drinking. Another ACOA told his alcoholic parents that they couldn't drink when they came into his house. Sometimes the first step is as simple as empowering the ACOA to put an end to phone conversations with a parent who is drunk.

Ironically, the situation is often not much easier for the ACOA if the alcoholic parent is no longer drinking. In this case, ACOAs may be reluctant to bring up the past drinking and its effects because they are afraid to upset the parent and precipitate a relapse. They may be immobilized by the feeling that they are supposed to be happy about their parent's sobriety while part of them bitterly protests that it's all "too little and too late." Additionally, it's often the case that sober parents cannot handle dealing with the past and will avoid addressing any of their children's hurt.

I treated one family in which the father dismissed his sons' anger about his outrageous behavior during his drinking years by saying to them that, since he was in recovery, he was putting the past behind him. Their anger, he said, was a manifestation of their "disease" a sign that they were still "stuck" in the past. The father could not deal with his sons' feelings about past episodes, such as the times he brought his dates into the house while his wife (their mother) lay dying upstairs in her bedroom. He couldn't face the past and the sons couldn't let go of it. The sober Dad was not a lot easier to deal with than the drunk Dad had been. In these cases, the first step is to validate the ACOAs' negative feelings about the parent's recovery and to encourage them to build a relationship with that parent without any expectations that it will make up for the past.

Obviously, the difficulty in dealing with a dead parent is that there is no direct way to come to a resolution. Death, however, does not end the relationship. The clinical challenge is to enable the client to work through that relationship and accept the ultimate lack of resolution.

If the parent is dead or still drinking and my client has given up trying to change him/her, then I encourage the clients to confront grief and anger directly by writing the parent an "I surrender" letter. The purpose of this letter is to allow the client openly to grieve the loss of hope that the relationship with the alcoholic parent will ever change. Since this letter is so difficult to write, many clients make several false starts. It is extremely important for the therapist not to rush the process, but to trust that working on this letter in and of itself is therapeutic. The value of the work transcends the product. Many clients find that writing merely "Dear Dad" or "Dear Mom" brings up enormous pain. The following are some excerpts from one client's I "surrender" letter.

Dear Dad,

(that sounds too personal)

I've never once written you a letter. It sounds almost artificially close and affectionate to write "dear." You were always on one side and us on the other. You made it that way. Your anger and your hostility leaked out of every word, out of every pore, out of every breath, and you weren't even aware of it. I remember being incredulous at your hurt that no one liked you.

You used to pull me to you when I was about five years old. You wanted to hug me. I'd pull and squirm away because I hated you even then. You were mean and loud, your face was rough with whiskers and you smelled of beer. I used to use your whiskers as an excuse to avoid getting near you, I didn't like their scratchiness. But there were some times when I let you hug me because I felt sorry for you. It was two things—you seemed so pathetic, wanting love from people and being rejected, or I'd sense that something was unfair, Ma was irrationally angry or something.

I remember once when it was just you and me one night at home and you made french fries from scratch. I can remember wanting you to connect with me so badly and it was like I was there making and eating french fries with a stranger. We had nothing to say to each other.

I was afraid of you. I used to sleep in that bottom bunk with three large dolls all around me, two on one side, one on the other, pressing in on me so I only had enough space to be straight in the bed. And I used to pile blankets on the bed no matter how hot it was. It was what I needed to feel safe. I never felt safe. There was nothing I could count on you were so unpredictable. I used to lie in bed and pray to some unknown God, pleading on the faintest glimmer of hope that there could be some change, that you wouldn't come home drunk, that you'd stop hating Jimmy. God! Jimmy! You detested him. Why did you hate Jimmy so much? That time he dumped the trash in the afternoon you wanted it dumped in the morning. Do you remember this? You never remembered anything and I remembered everything. I have to carry it around inside me and you never remembered.

The night of the "trash" we were all tense at the table. Bad things always happened at supper. I lost my appetite. I was so sick with fear. You were drunk. You started yelling at Jimmy, bullying him. You made him get up from the table to "talk" with him, you perverse bastard. You had only just gotten outside the kitchen into the hall when you started beating him up. Do you remember? There was a rumble, and you started punching him with those strong hairy destructive arms and to this day I am haunted by Jimmy's scream. It wasn't a scream of anger or for help, but one of terror, the same terror that I felt. Terror that you had turned on him, that you were out of control and that anything could happen. You could kill him. You wanted to kill him and Jimmy knew it. You, unpredictable, angry, drunk could do anything. No one could stop you. When it was over I left the table and got hysterical in the living room. I couldn't stop crying. They couldn't understand why I was so upset. I can remember Ma saying something about my being so sensitive. Do you remember me sitting on the living room floor hysterical because you came home drunk and beat up my brother because he emptied the trash in the afternoon rather than in the morning?

I wanted you to die. I always had the feeling that after you did something like this you felt satisfied, the same kind of satisfaction a fox might have after eating a rabbit, just doing what he had to do, a job well done, now time for some rest. You always went to bed after these "things." None of it ever seemed to mean anything to you.

(to continue)

I'm afraid to start writing again. It has taken me a week to get back to this. I'm afraid of the pain that goes with these words. I've started remembering my childhood, something I generally split off from and don't remember before the age of 17. I've started to remember that who I am today was founded on who I was then.

In my bedroom is a wastebasket lined with a paper bag. That bag has your writing on it, "Cupcake." That's what you called me. It was when I was sick and living in my apartment alone. I hadn't been over to the house for a couple of weeks and you sent me some of Ma's homemade chicken soup. That bag, that handwriting, was the last contact I had with you before you died. You're dead. I'm writing a letter to a dead person. You, my father, you're dead. I can't throw the bag out. The papers go in, I empty them out, more papers go in, but the bag stays.

I don't have anything else to say. It's over.

Anna

Death does not end a relationship. Hate does not cancel the yearning for love. Writing the letter does not heal the wound. It simply acknowledges it. The scar remains.

The next step involves helping the client understand the parent and the evolution of the alcoholism. ACOAs tend to have the image of the abusive, obnoxious drunk locked in their heads and to not have any sense of what their parent was like as a person. The best way to help clients fully appreciate the ravaging effects of the disease of alcoholism is for them to find out what their parent was like before he/she became an alcoholic.I encourage my clients to interview the alcoholic parent (when available), his spouse, his siblings, and even his parents about what he was like as a child and as a young adult before he became alcoholic. Our goal is to create a picture of the parent as a whole person with strengths and weaknesses.

One of my clients; Jeff, knew that his wealthy father had grown up in impoverished circumstances. However, when his Dad told him about having to go to school in torn and tattered secondhand clothes and being teased with the nickname "RagBoy," for the first time Jeff genuinely related to the intense anger and hurt that had fueled his ambition, his workaholism, and ultimately his alcoholism. No matter how successful he had become, his Dad never stopped feeling like "Rag Boy." Understanding the father as a person in his own context was a step toward making peace with the alcoholism.

Interviewing the alcoholic parent and the others who knew him is an effective way for my client to engage the parent on new terms. Usually the client has alternated between the hostile, reactive position and the trapped, enabling position; now he or she can initiate interaction with the parent as a curious historian. Since all people, including alcoholics, like to talk about themselves, this particular form of engaging the alcoholic parent is usually successful, although persistence is required.When the alcoholic parent is dead, interviewing friends and relatives is the primary avenue toward understanding the alcoholic as a person. I also encourage the client to bring in pictures of the alcoholic as a way of making him/her more real and accessible. Then I ask the client to engage in a dialogue with the picture of the alcoholic parent. For example, one man, looking at a photo of his father standing with his arm around the son at graduation, said:

> Dad, I love you and I feel terrible that so little of my life I got to spend with you as you might have been. I know that you couldn't help your problems with alcohol, but speaking as your son I would have wished that there were more moments when you and I were together like this. It just seems so unfair that when you finally stopped drinking you got sick and then you were in the hospital and then you were dead. It just seems so unfair.

One can feel this son's struggle to express his longing and love for his Dad, as well as his frustration and anger.

When alcoholic parents are invited to their adult children's therapy, extensive preparation is essential. My client needs to have all of his or her fantasies about resolution worked through, so that no great expectations are harbored. I conduct a low-key interview, making it clear that the parent's role is to be a consultant to me. Generally I ask all the questions while my client listens. This enables me to join the parent and make him/her feel comfortable. Then later, if my client does want to confront the parent in a session, the parent will feel safe enough with me to try it. I am careful to avoid unleashing years of my client's pent-up resentment, since that could lead to an irreparable rupture.

Clients are likely to be caught between the impulse to forgive and the deeply buried rage from childhood that blocks forgiveness. I differentiate between understanding the alcoholic and forgiving him for past destructive behavior. Wounds heal but scars last.

Working with the co-dependent parent. Clients usually have a variety of conflicted feelings about the co-dependent parent. On the one hand, the co-dependent is frequently seen as the parent who was emotionally available and provided what nurturance and support did exist in the family. On the other hand, the co-dependent was unable to protect the children from the alcoholic or to confront the alcoholism. ACOAs are usually quick to understand and forgive the co-dependent because they have had a much better relationship with this parent. They also look at the co-dependent's inability to deal with the alcoholism or violence from their own perspective of helplessness; therefore, they assume that the co-dependent is as much a legitimate victim as they were. While this is true, it ignores the difference between an adult who *does* not deal with destructive alcoholism and children who *cannot* deal with it. Part of coming to terms with the co-dependent is allowing oneself to feel the legitimate anger locked in the unasked question, "Why didn't you do something?"

While many ACOAs have difficulty being angry with the co-dependent parent, others blame and resent this parent even more than the alcoholic. It is not unusual for ACOAs who have thoroughly dismissed all feelings about the alcoholic to express anger at the co-dependent for her role in the family story. This is particularly true when the co-dependent was an active enabler who made excuses for the drinker's behavior and was in complete denial. I am treating one family in which the 80-year-old mother still refers to the father as someone who "was a little grouchy like the man in *Father Knows Best*," when in reality the father was violently abusive when drunk. The children, now in their fifties, are in a rage with their mother and her inability to acknowledge the reality of their lives.

The first step in coming to terms with the co-dependent parent is to address the stored-up resentment. Sometimes this means helping clients acknowledge their anger, and sometimes it means helping them let go of it. I usually ask clients to make a "resentment list" which basically addresses their anger at the parent for not having done anything about the alcoholism without the excuses that are normally employed by ACOAs to defuse their own anger.

The rest of the work involves the same interviewing process described above for dealing with the alcoholic parent. It is important for the ACOA to understand the co-dependent in terms of her history and particular context, to create a picture of the co-dependent as a child and young woman before she became trapped in the alcoholic marriage. Understanding the particular context in which the alcoholic marriage emerged also defuses any sense the client may have of being destined to follow in the parents' footsteps. The client learns to write a new family script.

I am currently working with a mother and daughter who are painstakingly addressing their mutual hurt and resentment about the roles they played in dealing with the alcoholic father/husband. During one session they were beginning to see how they had been trapped in the situation and ultimately pitted against each other in a rivalry over this man. The mother finally said to the daughter, "I know that I hurt you. I think I was really crazy at the time. When you got the other kids to confront him I just thought you were trying to wreck my marriage. I really resented you, especially when you kept seeing him after he left the house and started up with his girlfriend. That was the worst."

The daughter responded, "He was the only father I'm ever going to have. What would you expect? It was the first time in my life that he was ever sober and I'm not supposed to see him because it's going to hurt your feelings?"

The dialogue went on. The angry feelings and buried resentments poured out. Finally the daughter burst into tears and said, "I just wanted to have a father and mother without having to choose sides. Was that such a crime?" The mother moved over to the sofa and put her arms around her daughter. She didn't need to say anything at all.

Working with the child within. The last part of the family-of-origin work involves addressing the complicated and mixed feelings clients have about themselves as children growing up in dysfunctional or alcoholic families. It always surprises me how much blame ACOAs reserve for the kid they used to be. I'll never forget Anna telling me that it was her fault when her father beat up her brother because she was the one who told him that Jimmy didn't take out the trash when he was supposed to. I asked her how old she was at the time and she said, with no hint of self-awareness, "Oh, I was probably five, maybe six."

All the preceding work in relationship to siblings, alcoholic and co-dependent parents is designed to help ACOAs and their spouses develop some degree of empathy for themselves, as well as some appreciation for their lack of options and survival skills. Clients need to accept that, even though the defenses they developed as children have turned out to be self-defeating in adult life, they were useful at the time. Naturally, an emotionally deprived six-year-old might nurture herself with too much food, an abused boy might become a bully, and a scared eight-year-old might become painstakingly shy. After all, they were just kids.

Sometimes I ask clients to conjure up a mental picture of themselves as children under the age of 12 and imagine what they felt like, what their fears were, how hard they tried, how alone they felt. Then I ask them to consider just for a moment what they would like to give to that child if they could go back in time. These are some of their answers:

"I would tell her that it wasn't going to last forever."

"I would be his friend and we could play together."

"That it's okay she doesn't know how to make it better."

"A place she could go where she would be safe."

"Just a hug. That would be good enough."

"I would promise him that I will always love him."

There are a variety of ways to help the client nurture themselves more effectively. I encourage clients to develop some healthy indulgences, practice affirmations, accept their personality flaws, and learn how to grieve for their lost childhood. For example, I have one client who never expressed any of her feelings as a child and who survived by hiding behind a wall of silence. She's currently keeping a daily journal in which she takes herself back into childhood feeling and then writes them down. She brings the journal into the sessions and reads it. Slowly she's learning to let the little girl she used to be say the things that never got said.

Adult children bring themselves up the best that they can. Essentially I am teaching my clients how to be their own parent more effectively and lovingly.

As ACOAs separate their sense of an emerging adult self from the child they once were, they begin to feel more capable of taking risks. The key is recognizing that it is not up to your partner to take care of you and make life safe for you. That is something you do for yourself.

At this point we can work directly on the issues of intimacy and sexuality that brought the couple into the therapy. The work looks similiar to the last stage of the couples therapy I described in

Chapter 5, in which spouses learn how to risk becoming closer. Even as spouses allow themselves to begin trusting one another, I point out that one cannot be vulnerable without risking hurt. The difference is that they have a choice. As kids they couldn't fight and they couldn't flee. They had no choice. As adults they can *choose* to risk vulnerability in order to gain intimacy.

Jim and Cindy were in therapy for a year and a half. We had worked extensively on their families of origin. We had met with Cindy's siblings and even had a session with Jim's mother, who was now sober. In the course of therapy they had developed a deep empathic bond of appreciation for each other and their couple relationship.

After the family-of-origin work we focused on the sexual issues directly. Slowly they began to experiment with being more intimate with each other. When they arrived for one session it was obvious that they were both quite pleased with themselves and feeling somewhat shy. I asked them how they were doing, but they seemed a little uncomfortable being open. I suddenly had the feeling that their intimate life was none of my business. They had drawn a new boundary. It was time for me to get off the stage. Jim and Cindy had a marriage made in adulthood.

9

Therapist, Heal Thyself

This above all: to thine own self be true,
And it must follow, as the night the day,
Thou canst not then be false to any man.
Polonius/ *Hamlet,*
Act I, Scene III

Polonius is a politician and a diplomat, skilled at saying what others want to hear. He works on his agenda while appearing to be aligned with whatever faction is present. He speaks to his son about the virtues of being true to oneself and yet his actions seem to belie his words.

We are also politicians and diplomats. It is not our job to simply speak what's on our mind. We have to tailor our speech to fit our listeners' ability to hear. We skillfully go through the diplomatic gyrations of aligning with opposing factions. At what point do we risk losing ourselves? How do we integrate our values into our therapy? When should we express our beliefs at the risk of losing clients? At what point does maintaining therapeutic neutrality compromise our integrity as professionals and as people? When does joining and supporting a dysfunctional system become enabling?

Therapy is neither an art nor a science. It is just people working with people. We sweat. We worry. We do the best we can when we don't really know what we are doing. What does it mean to be true to oneself?

When my students present cases to me they inevitably provide me with detailed genograms and elaborate case histories. They focus on what's wrong with the family, where the family is stuck, and what strategies they've tried. Both in teaching and in conducting therapy, I frequently shift to the other end of the "bow tie" (Figure 1).

I want to know the expectations and pressures created by the forces on the righthand side of the bow tie. Each of these areas, from community norms to the therapist's unresolved conflicts, will have a profound impact on my assessment of the family and therapeutic goals. Who wants the treatment in the first place? What are the external pressures from the referral source or colleagues? How does my being a man affect the couple I'm treating? What about my own issues? What values and vulnerabilities are influencing me with a given family? My own reactivity must be evaluated as carefully as my client's. My internal reactions need to be considered along with everything else that is going on in the room. I can usually figure out what happened to me in a session after it's over. The real trick is tracking myself and my clients at the same time and knowing how to use my own responses selectively and therapeutically. I work on it every day.

When I teach about alcoholism and family therapy, I always ask the audience members about the extent of their personal connection to alcoholism. Invariably 80% indicate that they are either recovering from alcoholism, have been married to an alcoholic, or have grown up with an alcoholic parent. For most of us, having a personal connection to alcoholism is truly a mixed blessing.

Growing up in an alcoholic family is a form of on-the-job train-

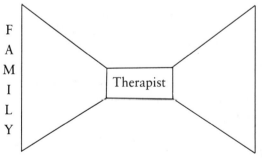

FIGURE 1   Therapist Bow Tie

ing for future clinicians. The survival skills one learns, e.g., to manage crises, to take care of others, and to work hard with little recognition, are often highly useful. For the child who struggled to keep the family functioning with little power and little success, becoming a therapist is quite attractive, since it provides the opportunity to be an acknowledged and powerful leader of families. In addition, being a therapist is also a potent way to experience an intense level of intimacy and closeness while staying in control. It is easier to be intimate on our time schedule and by our rules, safer to give love rather than to receive it.

Most of us in this field are in recovery. Clearly, we are not in this business for the money or the fame. We are in it because of our own life experiences, roles we played in our families, and our implicit need to "twelve step" as part of our healing. We all need to keep asking ourselves how we handle our own reactions, values, and feelings in relationship to our clients. How much is our empathy and ability to connect to the pain of others part of the problem rather than part of the solution? How do we know when feelings about our own struggles are impeding the therapy? Caring, commitment, and responsibility are all necessary ingredients of good therapy. How do we know when our caring becomes overinvolvement and our willingness to take responsibility becomes co-dependence?

These strong emotional undercurrents result in a high potential for intense reactivity in our work. Sometimes we try to rescue families in spite of themselves. Sometimes we are distant and punitive. In some cases we become enablers, inadvertently reinforcing the denial in the family. In other cases we blow family members out of treatment with a confrontation that is "for their own good."

I get caught in all these positions. One week I'm trying to rescue the family and the next week, since no one has changed, I move toward confrontation. If that doesn't work, I might feel guilty and move back toward the rescuing position. I frequently get the sense that I'm working harder than the family. This is not good. Sometimes, I wish someone would say to me, "David, take two Al-Anons and get plenty of bed rest."

Many therapists attempt to suppress the feeling responses that are uncomfortable for them. This just pushes the feelings into the unconscious. They still are played out in the therapy. When we are bothered by a client, it shows, whether we acknowledge our feeling to ourselves or not. The person of the therapist is never outside the system. Regardless of the type of case or our personal background, we all have to deal with fear, self-doubt, confusion, and feelings of inadequacy.

KNOTS

Diane had a knot in her stomach as she sat with the family during the first session. The father seemed to have alcohol on his breath. When she had greeted the family in the waiting room, the father had leered at her and said, "Well now, isn't this a surprise. I didn't expect the doctor to be such a pretty young lady." She had smiled weakly and felt suddenly afraid. Diane felt the session was going badly. She kept trying to engage the father and the mother in working on what to do about their son's school phobia. She was trying to establish a parental hierarchy. The mother simply wrung her hands and said that she didn't know what to do. The father kept asking her personal questions, such as whether or not she had children of her own. Diane found herself answering his questions in spite of herself. She felt afraid. She was mad at herself for feeling afraid and worried that she was showing her fear. She wasn't sure whether this man was baiting her or just being inappropriately friendly or both. When the father asked her whether she had a man in her life, Diane heard herself lying to him. "Yes, I do," she answered.

Suddenly, Diane found herself remembering being eight years old and her Dad screaming at her, accusing her of having hidden the whiskey bottles. She lied to him, saying that she didn't know where the whiskey was. He knew she was lying. He pinned her against the wall and began to slap her. Finally she told him where the bottles were and he dropped her. She collapsed on the floor like a broken doll.

She refocused her attention on the session. The knot in her stomach felt worse. Her mouth was dry. Her heart was pounding. She kept thinking about what she was supposed to say. She didn't know what to say. She just wanted the session to be over.

Fortunately, most of us don't have flashbacks in the middle of sessions, but we all feel scared and immobilized from time to time.

Substance abusers can be very intimidating. Sometimes they are out of control, potentially dangerous, and hostile toward the therapist. Sometimes they are so smooth and skilled at colluding and denial that the therapist begins to feel anxious about what is real and what isn't. Growing up in an alcoholic family means doubting one's own perceptions, being afraid, and feeling out of control. It is not surprising that, when we are treating these same kinds of families, we sometimes feel the old helplessness and fear from our childhoods. After nearly 20 years of working with these families, I can still feel like an overwhelmed beginner in the middle of a session.

In Control

Dr. Bob Mclure is well liked and respected by both his patients and his collegues. He is an excellent psychiatrist and always has a "cool head" in a crisis. He's always in control. Dr. Mclure is an individual therapist and most of his patients are adults who are exhibiting some symptoms of depression and/or anxiety. In addition to being clinically skilled, Dr. Mclure is quite knowledgeable about psychopharmacology and treats most of his patients with either antidepressants or tranquilizers combined with intensive psychodynamic psychotherapy.

Dr. Mclure's stance on substance abuse is quite clear. If the client is an alcoholic, then he suspends treatment until he or she goes into AA. Usually the client just drops out of treatment. If the patient acknowledges a moderate dependency on substances but is basically functioning adequately, Dr. Mclure will work with him/her to sort through the underlying dynamics that may be creating stress and the need to use chemicals. Many of his patients simply never mention how much they drink, and, since Dr. Mclure is nondirective, he doesn't bring it up.

Bob Mclure is also in control of his use of chemicals. He limits himself to three drinks a night and he's careful not to drive home after a party if he's had a little too much to drink. Bob is particularly careful about drugs because he saw what they did to his mother. Her chronic depression was clearly exacerbated by her dependency on Valium and barbiturates. Bob would never prescribe drugs for himself and he's quite careful about not relying on his wife's Valium too often when he has trouble falling asleep.

Clearly most of us who specialize in the substance abuse field have had to confront our own chemical use. All of us who come from substance abuse backgrounds are at risk. Being therapists does not inoculate us against the dangers. Bob Mclure has a blind spot about his own carefully regulated dependency on alcohol, which makes it highly unlikely that he will recognize and confront the similiar patterns in his patients.

In her book, *Another Chance*, Sharon Wegscheider-Cruse refers to the notion of the "professional enabler," someone who inadvertently reinforces the family pattern because of his or her own unresolved issues. Bob is caught in that role. He treats people individually, so he is dependent on their candor about their use of chemicals without input from family members. His reliance on the use of drugs to treat depression and anxiety may mask clients' dependence on alcohol or their difficulties with a spouse/parent who is an alcoholic. Finally, Bob's own pattern of alcohol use, while not overtly problematic for him, reduces his sensitivity to moderate substance abuse in his patients.

Bob Mclure's blind spots may seem reassuringly obvious to us, and yet none of us is immune from our own areas of vulnerability when we practice therapy. It's the nature of being a therapist that we often treat issues that we have not resolved in our own lives. I am mindful of the ease with which I teach parents about how to set limits with their children, only to discover that I have difficulty being consistent with my own sons. I tell parents to administer judicious punishments rather than using anger to control children; however, I often resort to anger in dealing with my own children. I was painfully reminded of this last year when I hosted a radio talk show on parenting issues. Naturally I dispensed bright, pithy, and useful advice. When I arrived home, I discovered that my nine-year-old son was not impressed. In fact, the babysitter had to discourage him from calling during the show to ask me on the air why I lost my temper so much. "Practice what you preach, Dad," can be a hard rule to follow.

TOUGH

Everyone at the treatment center knows that Ellen is tough. Behind her back some of the men call her "the drill sergeant" with a mixture of fear and respect. She's never afraid to nail someone to the wall for "bullshitting about their addiction." She hates it when patients waste time complaining about their families or their difficult past. She calls it "damn excusifying" and tells them to "get off the pity pot and get with the program." Ellen's patients know that she will always be there for them. Even though she's tough, she's always around for a little extra one on one. The patients can't wait to get into her group. It's considered an honor to be "waxed, polished, and Ellenized." Ellen's tough honesty, commitment to her groups, and dedication to the program make her a powerful role model for the staff as well as the patients.

Ellen's parents both died before she got sober. Her brother lives in Hawaii. Her ex-husband is remarried and has started a new family. Her son is a doctor and lives on the opposite coast.

Once a year Ellen goes to visit her son and the grandchildren. The visits are awkward. Her son and his wife drink wine with dinner. When they ask Ellen if she minds, she reassures them that it's all right. They don't smoke, so Ellen has to sneak off to the porch for a cigarette. She and her son never talk about the past. In fact, they don't talk about much of anything. Ellen's daughter-in-law is very reserved and only talks about the kids. Ellen tries to be very nice with the twins, but they are teenagers now and don't have much time for their grandmother. Each year Ellen tells her friends in the program that she's not going back, but she always does.

Ellen works six days a week, goes to a lot of meetings, and lives alone.

Since working with drug addiction and alcoholism demands an intense level of commitment, therapists like Ellen frequently make the critical difference in setting some patients on the road to recovery. One of the most compelling attributes that a therapist can bring to the addictions field is his/her personal history of recovering from an addiction. Yet this is truly a double-edged sword. On the one hand, Ellen's sobriety sets a shining example for others; on the other, Ellen may be prone to overidentify with her clients and to project too much of her own experience and her own solutions onto them.

What about Ellen's continuing recovery? How dependent has she become on her patients to replace her family and to meet her needs for intimacy and feelings of self-worth? To what extent does confronting her patients' concerns about their families and their past reflect her own alienation from her family and avoidance of her past? Ellen may be at a developmental impasse. Her emotional isolation is assuaged by turning to her clients rather than dealing with her loneliness.

Sometimes being in therapy is what people do to avoid change. Sometimes being a therapist is a way to avoid oneself. We all have our moments of hiding out in the therapist's chair. Every once and a while, I consider the possibility that I won't really complete my recovery until I have recovered from being a therapist.

On-the-Job Training

When my mother finally stopped drinking, she lay in bed most of the time. She read books. My father and I brought her food on the tray. One morning we tried to cheer her up by doing a soft shoe dance step together as we came into the room with the tray. She smiled.

I had never spent time with my father before. He had always been too busy. But I was the only kid still at home and Mom wasn't cooking so Dad and I went out to dinner a lot. We would talk about Mom. We always ate at this cheap steak house around the corner from our house. The food was terrible, but I liked it anyway. I liked listening to my Dad talk about my Mom. I even gave advice.

One night, my mother and my father were "having a disagreement" (they never "fought"). My mother was in the bedroom and my father was downstairs in the library. I spent time with one; then I would go and sit with the other one. I offered my mother some advice. She turned to me and said, "Why don't you mind your own goddamn business!"

It felt like a slap in the face. I felt small. I went to my room.

During my first year as a therapist at Eagleville Hospital I had a chance to work with Jesse. It was his ninth admission. Jesse came into treatment every year in January when it was cold. He had a voluminous file and almost everyone at the hospital knew his story. He had been brought up in the hills of West Virginia, where he had been kept like a dog. For several years he had been locked in a shed in the backyard and fed only table scraps. He was beaten on a daily basis in order to ensure that that the devil wouldn't want him.

I read the record and decided that I would be the one to get to Jesse. Every day in group we worked over Jesse, trying to get him in touch with his feelings. He was always cheerful and compliant, but he expressed some concern that maybe he was using up too much of the group's time.

On the first warm day in March, Jesse was caught trying to walk off the grounds with his suitcase. I called an emergency group session. We spent eight hours confronting Jesse. We screamed at him and cried for him. Jesse seemed oblivious to it all; however, I was sure he was just on the verge of cracking him. Finally the other group members insisted that we give up and let him go. I got mad at them and called them a bunch of cold-hearted bastards, while Jesse quietly slipped out of the room. I caught up with him and suggested that I give him a ride to town, so that we could talk it through one on one.

All the way to Norristown I kept hammering at him about saving his life and how much I cared. When we got to Norristown Jesse directed me to a deserted street, nothing but gutted, empty houses. He asked me to let him out. When I asked him why he wanted to get out on this empty street, he turned and said, "Well, Dave, I just thought it would be better if you dropped me off here, because around the corner is my favorite bar and I just didn't want you to have to watch me walk into it."

Jesse was also telling me to mind my own business.

Many of us in the substance abuse field are former parental children in our family of origin. Instead of retiring, we have continued to play out our old family scripts by becoming professional "heros." We are often painfully aware of repeating these old roles with our spouses, children, and clients.

Being therapists meets significant emotional needs in our lives. For many of us, closeness in the therapy room is easier than intimacy with our spouses, our parents and siblings, or our children. Our role is more clearly defined. We are more in control. It is safer. It is very disconcerting to discover that it is easier for me to connect on a deep emotional level with my clients' pain about their childhoods than to be in touch with my own. It is disconcerting for me to be able to provide gentle and loving nurturance for my clients and yet have difficulty letting myself be nurtured by the people who love me.

Paradoxically, the people we treat are often so dysfunctional and out of control that they need us to be our naturally overresponsible, co-dependent selves. Drowning people are not rescued by swimming lessons. Someone has to be willing to get in the water with them and pull them out. When does rescuing save a life and when does it keep someone from learning how to swim? If the person we rescue won't take lessons and keeps jumping back in the pool, how many times should we jump in after them? When was the right time to let Jesse go?

I don't have any easy answers to these questions. For any given individual case at any given time the answers may be different. Many of us err by caring too much. Some of us err by caring too little. I assume that I will never get it just right. I would rather risk caring too much.

Diane's fear, Bob's denial and enabling, Ellen's projection and dependency, as well as my own overfunctioning, are examples of how we sometimes express our unresolved issues in the therapy room. Most of us are still working on our recovery. Mike Elkin isn't that far off when he jokes, "Therapists are the only people around who need 25 hours of therapy per week." When you're a therapist, part of recovery is accepting that you will always make mistakes, that the more you know the more you'll realize how much you don't know, and that recovery takes forever. Our obligation is to learn from our mistakes, stay attuned to our own issues, and resist taking ourselves too seriously. We need to be able to experience the joy of tears and tears of joy.

On my first day at Eagleville Hospital, my supervisor, Robert Klein, said to me that the most important thing in therapy was having fun. At the time I was affronted by this facetious remark. It turns out he was right. It has to be fun.

Epilogue

HOMEWARD BOUND

I learned about smiling before I was five. They all would smile back, but they never see me at all. I could sit behind my smile and just watch.

I remember being little on early April days when there were still patches of snow and the ground was wet and squishy. The air had a chill in it but the sun was warm on my face as I walked down the hill to the pine trees. I would find a place where the pine needles were dry. Then I would lie on my back and watch the clouds move across the sky. I would breathe in the smell of pine and listen to the wind rustling through the trees. It felt good to be alone. It made me feel big and small at the same time. I didn't need to smile.

*   *   *   *   *

My mother was cold sober when she killed herself. She had been treated by the best. They gave her a lot of pills. They never treated her for the alcoholism. She gave up the drinking on her own. The pills were supposed to help her. On the last day, she took them all so there would be no mistake.

For a long time I felt dead inside and I wrote cold poems.

> To Mother
> You squat on my days
> like some obscene hen
> smothering her young.
>
> Sometimes I think
> that you forget
> that you are dead.
>   1968

I became the family caretaker and I became a therapist. I learned to feel by taking care of others' feelings. I learned to grieve by borrowing others' tears.

A few years ago, when I was working on my family-of-origin issues, I got my family together for a weekend retreat. To one and all I announced, in a somewhat self-righteous and self-pitying monologue, that it was high time I stopped being the family caretaker, that I needed to take care of my own needs, and that they should all take care of themselves. Much to my surprise, they all said "fine."

Everyone is doing much better now that I've retired.

*   *   *   *   *

They sat in my office and said nothing, two sisters, a brother, and a brother-in-law. Their silence was heavy and thick. They didn't look at each other or me. Their eyes shifted restlessly around the room. The week before their brother had died. He had killed himself.

One brother was barely functioning, having spent the past ten years in and out of psychiatric hopitals. The sister and her husband had a marriage that was slowly disintegrating. The other sister lived alone and tried to take care of her siblings and the two aging but actively alcoholic parents. I had been involved in treating all of them at one point or another. I had helped them believe that they needed to live their own lives and stop devoting themselves to trying to rescue family members in trouble. I had taught them about co-dependency and enabling. They had all been making progress.

In the days before the brother killed himself he had called each one of them and, through a drunken haze, asked them to come and help him. He had made these desperate phone calls for years and years. They had always come. They had dragged him off to hospitals. But his recovery was always temporary. It wouldn't take him long to return to the coke and the booze. This time each of the siblings did the "right" thing. They all refused his demands. They told him that they would support him only if he took the first step and put himself into treatment. He killed himself instead.

One of the sisters finally spoke. As she did the tears began to run down her face, "I thought we were all going to be okay. He seemed better this summer. We all seemed better. I thought the worst was over. I remember saying to him when he was just a little boy and he was crying in my arms after father had beaten him, 'Don't worry, Johnny. We're all going to grow up someday and we'll get away from this house and it will all be okay. Daddy'll never be able to hurt us again once we're all grown up.'"

I didn't know what to say. But I've finally learned that I don't always have to know what to say.

*   *   *   *   *

My office is in my home. From it I can look out over the backyard and see the swingset among the pine trees. After school my son likes to get on the swings. Out of the corner of my eye I can watch him. He swings very high. Then he just sits there and doesn't swing at all. Occasionally, when I get a break, I go out there and sit with him. We don't talk much. We just sit and listen to the wind in the trees.

*   *   *   *   *

Well, Mom, the book's done. It's called *Before It's Too Late*. I wish you could read it. Actually, I don't care that much about you reading the book. I just wish you were here.

1988

Bibliography

Ackerman, R. J. (1979). *Children of alcoholics*. Holmes Beach, FL: Learning Publications.

Ackerman, R. J. (1986). *Growing in the shadow*. Pompano Beach, FL: Health Communications Inc.

Ackerman, R. J. (1987). *Same house, different child*. Pompano Beach, FL: Health Communications Inc.

Andolfi, M. (1979). *Family therapy: An interactional approach*. New York: Plenum Press.

Andolfi, M., Angelo, C., Menghi, P., & Nicolo-Corigliaro, A. M. (1983). *Behind the family mask*. New York: Brunner/Mazel.

Bateson, G. (1972). *Steps to an ecology of mind*. New York: Chandler Publishing Company.

Bean, M. & Zinberg, N. (Eds.). (1981). *Dynamic approaches to the understanding and treatment of alcoholism*. New York: Free Press.

Bepko, C. with Krestan, J. (1985). *The responsibility trap: A blueprint for treating the alcoholic family*. New York: The Free Press.

Berenson, D. (1976a). A family approach to alcoholism. *Psychiatry Opinion, 13:* 33–38.

Berenson, D. Alcohol and the family system. In P. Geurin (Ed.), *Family therapy: Theory and practice*. New York: Gardner Press.

Berenson, D. The therapist's relationship with couples with an alcoholic member. In E. Kaufman & P. Kaufman (Eds.), *Family therapy of drug and alcohol abuse*. New York: Gardner Press.

Bergman, J. S. (1985). *Fishing for barracuda*. New York: W. W. Norton.

Black, C. *It will never happen to me*. Denver, CO: M.A.C.

Bowen, M. (1978). *Family therapy in clinical practice*. Northvale, NJ: Jason Aronson.

Carnes, P. (1987). *Out of the shadows: Treating sexual addiction.* Minneapolis: CompCare Publications.

Davis, D. I., Berenson, D., Steinglass, P., & Davis, S. (1974). The adaptive consequences of drinking. *Psychiatry, 37*: 209–215.

De Shazer, S. (1982). *Patterns of brief family therapy.* New York: Guilford.

Dulfano, C. (1982). *Families, alcoholism and recovery: Ten stories.* Center City, MN: Hazelden Educational Services.

Elkin, M. (1984). *Families under the influence.* New York: W. W. Norton.

Figley, C. R. (Ed.). (1985). *Trauma and its wake.* New York: Brunner/Mazel.

Fossum, M. & Mason, M. J. (1982). *Facing shame: Families in recovery.* New York: W. W. Norton.

Haley, J. (1976). *Problem solving therapy.* San Francisco: Jossey-Bass.

Haley, J. (1980). *Leaving home.* New York: McGraw-Hill.

Herman, J. (1981). *Father-daughter incest.* Cambridge: Harvard University Press.

Jackson, J. (1954). The adjustment of the family to the crisis of alcoholism. *Quarterly Journal of Studies on Alcohol, 15*, 4: 562–586.

Jellenik, E. M. (1960). *The disease concept of alcoholism.* New Haven, CT: College and University Press.

Johnson, V. (1973). *I'll quit tomorrow.* New York: Harper & Row.

Kaufman, E. & Kaufman, P., (Eds.). (1979). *Family therapy of drug and alcohol abuse.* New York: Gardner Press.

Kellerman, J. (1976). *Alcoholism: A merry-go-round named denial.* Center City, MN: Hazelden Educational Services.

Kurtz, E. (1979). *Not-God: A history of Alcoholics Anonymous.* Center City, MN: Hazelden Educational Services.

Lawson, G., Peterson, J. & Lawson, A. (1983). *Alcoholism and the family.* MD: Aspen.

Lewis, J. M., Beavers, W. R., Gossett, J. T., & Phillips, V. A. (1976). *No single thread: Psychological health in family systems.* New York: Brunner/Mazel.

Maxwell, R. (1976). *The booze battle.* New York: Ballantine Books.

Maxwell, R. (1986). *Breakthrough.* New York: Ballantine Books.

Middleton-Moz, J. & Dwinell, L. (1986). *After the tears.* Pompano Beach, FL: Health Communications.

Minuchin, S. (1974). *Families and family therapy.* Cambridge: Harvard University Press.

Morawetz, A. & Walker, G. (1984). *Brief therapy with single-parent families.* New York: Brunner/Mazel.

Sager, C. J., Brown, H. S., Crohn, H., Engel, T., Rodstein, E., & Walker, L. (1983). *Treating the remarried family.* New York: Brunner/Mazel.

Schaef, A. W. (1986). *Co-dependence: Misunderstood—mistreated.* San Francisco, CA: Harper & Row.

Selvini Palazzoli, M., Boscolo, L., Cecchin, G., & Prata, G. (1980). Hypothesizing-circularity-neutrality: Three guidelines for conductor of the session. *Family Process, 19*(1): 3–12.

Sexias, J. & Youcha, G. (1986). *Children of alcoholism: A survivor's manual.* New York: Harper & Row.

Sobell, M. & Sobell, L. (Eds.). *Emerging concepts of alcohol dependence.* New York: Springer.

Stanton, M. D., Todd, T. C., & Associates. (1982). *The family therapy of drug abuse and addiction.* New York: Guilford.

Steinglass, P. (1979). Family therapy with alcoholics: A review. In E. Kaufman & P. N. Kaufman (Eds.). *Family therapy of drug and alcohol abuse* (pp. 147–186). New York: Gardner Press.

Steinglass, P., Davis, D. I., & Berenson, D. (1977). Observations of con-jointly hospitalized alcoholic couples during sobriety and intoxication: Implications for theory and therapy. *Family Process, 16:* 1–16.

Vaillant, G. (1983). *The natural history of alcoholism.* Cambridge: Harvard University Press.

Van der Kolk, B. (1987). *Psychological trauma.* Washington, DC: American Psychiatric Press, Inc.

Wallace, J. (1977). Alcoholism from the inside out. In N. J. Estes & M. E. Heinemann (Eds.). (1981). *Alcoholism: Development, consequences and interventions.* St. Louis: Mosby.

Walsh, F. (Ed.). (1982). *Normal family processes.* New York: Guilford.

Wegscheider-Cruse, S. (1981). *Another chance: Hope and health for the alcoholic family.* Palo Alto, CA: Science and Behavior Books.

Whitfield, C. (1983). *Healing the child within.* Pompano Beach, FL: Health Communications, Inc.

Woititz, J. G. (1983). *Adult children of alcoholics.* Pompano Beach, FL: Health Communications, Inc.

Woititz, J. G. (1985). *Struggle for intimacy.* Pompano Beach, FL: Health Communications, Inc.

Index